Smiling Through Your Tears: Anticipating Grief

Copyright 2004 by Harriet Hodgson and Lois Krahn, MD.
All rights reserved.
Cover photo by Helen Welby, BE, MBA. Copyright 2004 by Helen Welby. All rights reserved.
Published by BookSurge LLC, 5341 Dorchester Road, Suite 16, North Charleston, South Carolina, 29418. Internet address www.booksurge.com.
The information contained in this book is not intended to serve as a replacement for professional medical advice. Any use of the information in this book is at the reader's discretion. The authors and the publisher specifically disclaim any and all liability arising directly or indirectly from the use or application of any information contained in this book. A medical professional should be consulted regarding your specific situation.

Printed in the United States of America.
ISBN: 1-59457-932-6

Library of Congress Control Number: 2005902737

To order additional copies, please contact us.
BookSurge, LLC
www.booksurge.com
1-866-308-6235
orders@booksurge.com

HARRIET HODGSON, BS, MA &
LOIS KRAHN, MD

SMILING THROUGH YOUR TEARS: ANTICIPATING GRIEF

BookSurge LLC
2004

Smiling Through Your Tears: Anticipating Grief

CONTENTS

A Heartfelt Thank You	ix
Acknowledgements	xi
Preface	xiii
Chapter 1: What Makes Early Grief Unique?	1
Chapter 2: The Early Grief of Terrorism	19
Chapter 3: Grief as a Reaction to Change	33
Chapter 4: Factors That Shape Early Grief	51
Chapter 5: Early Grief's Symptoms and Stages	67
Chapter 6: Responses to Early Grief	83
Chapter 7: When Early Grief Gets Complicated	103
Chapter 8: Adding to Your Coping Skills	121
Chapter 9: How Early Grief May Help You	139
Conclusion	157
Appendix A: Words to Know	163
Appendix B: More Reading	169
About the Authors	179

A HEARTFELT THANK YOU

We are grateful to the people who shared their stories with us. Thank you for your courage, your wisdom, and your practical tips. Though your names have been changed to protect your privacy, the truth of your stories is unchanged, and shines like stars in the night sky. Like the stars, your stories will help others to navigate and find their way through early grief.

Harriet and Lois

Acknowledgements

This book wouldn't have a happy sunflower on the cover were it not for my daughter, Helen Welby, and her 12-year-old twins, Haley and John. Finding a photo for a book about early grief was a challenge, to say the least. A photo of a smiling or crying person was too obvious for me. What could I do? I purchased a sunflower from a garden shop and called my daughter. "Would you photograph a sunflower for me?" I asked.

"I'd be glad to," she replied, and promised to bring her digital camera along when she and the twins came for dinner. The sun was just starting to go down when we went out on the deck to take photos. Haley and John took turns holding the sunflower against various backgrounds, but the backgrounds were busy and the light wasn't right, so they moved to the front of the house.

I asked Helen to photograph the sunflower against the blue sky. My grandson lay on the sidewalk and held the sunflower, which was as large as a dinner plate, over his head. To get the right camera angle my daughter stretched out on her tummy beside him. Our house is on a corner and driver after driver slowed down to stare at the sight – a prostrate boy with a sunflower over his head, a determined mother with a camera, and a young girl dancing around.

As you can see, their efforts paid off, and I thank my daughter and grandchildren for their help. I also thank my husband, John, for proofreading the manuscript and for his unfailing support during 12 years of writing. Thanks to Johnson printing in Rochester, MN for its technical assistance with the photo. Last, and far from least, I thank my co-author, Dr. Lois Krahn, for believing in this book.

Harriet Hodgson

PREFACE

*Time heals griefs and quarrels,
for we change and are no longer the same person.*

Pascal, 1670

Early grief is a feeling of loss before a death or dreaded event occurs. Though anticipatory grief is the correct medical term for this process, it's a mouthful to say and read, so we use early grief instead. Millions of people deal with this kind of grief every day, yet little has been written about it. Maybe that's because we don't like to think about sad things.

But early grief is part of life and touches us all. Harriet Hodgson, a nonfiction writer for 26 years, and Dr. Lois Krahn, a Mayo Clinic psychiatrist, think there is a growing need for information about early grief. Each of them reached this conclusion for different reasons. Harriet's conclusion comes from life experience.

When her husband was an Air Force Flight Surgeon he was sent to Vietnam for a year and she wasn't sure he would come home alive. Years later, her daughter was nearly killed in a car crash. Her daughter's injuries were so severe – a broken neck, blood clot on the brain, and wedged back vertebrae – Harriet feared she would die. But there are real miracles in life and her daughter survived.

Later in life Harriet became her mother's caregiver. For nine years her mother suffered from probable Alzheimer's disease and the demands of caregiving increased daily. No matter how hard she tried, Harriet couldn't meet these demands, and she became stressed and depressed. She didn't know how long these feelings would last, how disabled her mother would become, or how she would feel after she died. Still, Harriet made the most of her mother's final days and kept smiling through her tears.

More recently, her husband's aorta split in two, a life-threatening event. Thanks to the quick response of the emergency medical team her husband beat the odds and lived. Physicians treated her husband successfully with medication for years, but knew he would eventually need major, life-threatening surgery. Early grief lingered in the shadows of his life and Harriet's life as well.

All of these uncertainties were terrible to deal with and Harriet wondered at her responses to them. What was going on? She read articles from the Medline database, books about early grief, and talked with people who had experienced it. Slowly a book idea took shape in Harriet's mind and she wrote a chapter-by-chapter outline. She was unable to start the book, however, because caring for her mother took over her life.

After her mother's death in 1997 Harriet could see her early grief journey more clearly. She wrote a new outline and turned to Lois Krahn for medical advice. Lois read the outline carefully. "I love your book!" she exclaimed. Her reaction touched Harriet deeply because it showed that Lois saw the outline as a published book. The reaction also validated Harriet's life experience.

Though they lived in the same neighborhood Lois, the mother of two young children and Harriet, the grandmother of twins, had never met. On this project they had a meeting of the minds. Lois had her own reasons for being interested in the book.

During her career as a psychiatrist she had encountered early grief many times and in different settings. Reading Harriet's outline made Lois think of the people she has known who dreaded certain life events that hadn't happened yet. She, too, has seen families struggle with a parent afflicted with Alzheimer's and the early grief that comes with this experience.

One man had medical problems related to AIDS. Another patient, a three-year old child, had a recurrence of cancer, which was unlikely to respond to treatment. A soon-to-be mother was diagnosed with cancer in the last months of pregnancy. Lois and Harriet can give you more examples, but you get the idea; both are well acquainted with early grief.

Early grief may strike at any time and for different reasons. You may grieve for an aging parent who suffered a debilitating stroke. You may grieve when you find out that your company is downsizing and, according to the rumor mill, 150 jobs will be cut. You may grieve when you and your partner start divorce proceedings.

Stress may keep you from recognizing your early grief and that's OK. Confronting feelings is often painful and you may come up with excuses to explain your feelings. You may tell yourself that you're overtired, overworked, and feeling blue. Sure, early grief can make you tired, muddle your mind, and make you feel blue, but it's more complicated than that. Research findings suggest that early grief is as raw and powerful as "normal" grief. That makes it a big deal. You may feel early grief if your:

- baby is born with a heart defect
- teenager is hooked on drugs
- loved one is in the military and receives orders for a combat zone
- partner has threatened suicide
- retirement date is approaching
- dear friend is dying of AIDS
- parent is in a hospice
- life involves caring for the chronically or terminally ill
- government raises the terror alert

This book focuses on early grief before death and guides you through the process. It's designed to be reader friendly. Each chapter begins with a quotation to help you focus your thoughts. Topical headings guide you through the text. Stories from people who've experienced early grief bring research findings to life. Healing steps – 114 of them in all – are printed in bold within the text and summarized at the end of the chapters.

One by one, these healing steps lead you to your healing path. The reading time for this book is about three hours. You don't have to read it all at one sitting. Read the parts you need most first and save the rest for later. Tears are cleansing and if you feel like crying while you read go ahead and do it. Early grief is part of the human experience. Though you can't avoid it, you can get through it, and create a new and meaningful life.

CHAPTER 1
What Makes Early Grief Unique?

As long as we feel hope, there is hope.

Harriet Goldhor Lerner, PhD

SMILING THROUGH YOUR TEARS: ANTICIPATING GRIEF

Early grief hasn't received much publicity so you may think you know nothing about it. But if you saw the television coverage of the terrorist attacks on the World Trade Center in New York City, the plane crash in Pennsylvania, and the gaping hole in the Pentagon in Washington, DC, you know lots about it. You saw the shock on people's faces, the immense cloud of cement ash and flying debris, the licking flames of fire, and the twisted structural steel.

And you mourned with the victims' families. Perhaps you belong to one of these families and grieve for a loved one, friend, or colleague. Like the great wars and other catastrophic events, September 11th, 2001 will be a marker in human history. On this day approximately 3,000 families associated with the World Trade Center began their early grief journey. A short time later, people who had ties with the plane crash in Pennsylvania and the Pentagon were also grieving.

No one expected to take this journey, yet they were on it together. In New York City, family members taped posters of their loved ones in phone booths, on the windshields of crushed cars, and on a display that became known as the Wall of Hope. According to journalist Elizabeth LeSure, voicing the names of the missing was a mantra "repeated to volunteers, over hot lines, on television."

Hope was the common theme of these messages. Until they were certain a loved one or friend had died these courageous people hoped their loved ones were alive. "I just want my husband to come home," a wife said. "If he is injured we will take care of him." Family members and friends continued their search despite overwhelming feelings of early grief.

Early grief changed them and it changed our nation. What is early grief? How does it affect you? Why is it so painful? How do you cope with it? Can you get your life back on track? Will your life ever be the same?

Dr. Eric Lindemann, a psychiatrist, was the first person to define early grief. The year was 1940. His description was based on observations of 101 patients, including survivors of the 1942 Coconut Grove Nightclub fire in Boston, MA. Ruth Hurber, PhD and John W. Bigson, DSW cite Lindemann's research in their article, "New Evidence for Anticipatory Grief."

"Lindemann observed that patients who had a forewarning of imminent death reacted differently when the death actually occurred than those for whom death was totally unexpected," they write.

Forewarning is the key word here. Early grief starts the minute you hear the awful news. When you think about it, this is a logical response. Humans have imaginative minds and we can visualize someone's death, the void it will leave in our lives, and the pain we will feel afterwards. Though we manage to cope, the struggle is constant, and our early grief keeps getting worse.

Focuses of Early Grief

The focuses of grief may shift, yet you are always dealing with them. Grief expert Therese A. Rando, PhD says early grief has three focuses: past, present, and future. Unfortunately, your thoughts may jump from one focus to another. The fragmented thoughts that come to your mind are confusing and worrisome. Friends may think you're "whacko."

You may start to worry about yourself. One minute you are writing a loved one's obituary and the next minute you're planning a weekend trip with your loved one. Mixing the present with the past is painful because of the collage of hope, guilt, and grief. It's hard to know what to plan for—the present or the future. Plans may also change at the last minute.

Still, there are ways you can help yourself. One is to **be aware of the focuses of early grief.** There may be days when you feel more comfortable thinking about the past than the present. What are your thoughts now? Being aware of the focuses of early grief takes effort, but it will help you to put your life in context.

Accept the fact that there is no away around grief. The only way to get over grief is to experience it. This means you live with emotional pain. Once you accept the fact that there is no way around grief, you may channel more energy towards coping with it. It will be easier to cope with early grief if you know the factors that make it unique, starting with uncompleted loss.

Uncompleted Loss

Every day is a day of uncompleted loss for those who are going through early grief. In her classic work, *Death and Dying*, Elizabeth Kubler-Ross notes that early grief differs from the grief that follows death because the loss isn't final. What's more, you don't know when your loss will be final. Life becomes a waiting game.

Circular emotions are the result of uncompleted loss. You may go from early grief, to acceptance of loss, and back to early grief again. Like a car that's out of alignment, your life is out of alignment, off-balance and difficult to steer. Indeed, you may not know where you're going. Getting back on track will be a challenge.

"The process of regaining balance is complicated because the loss is not final," explain Beatrice Turkoski, PhD, RN and Brenda Lance, MSN, RN, authors of "The Use of Guided Imagery With Anticipatory Grief." Though your loss isn't final you may be able to steady your life.

For 10 years Henry had been concerned about his wife, who had Alzheimer's disease. When her disease was first diagnosed Henry, a medical professional, was convinced he could handle things. He had researched the disease extensively and seen Alzheimer's patients. But as his wife's disease progressed it became harder for Henry to cope. The day came when his wife needed more medical support than Henry could provide. And so, with great sadness and love, he moved her to an assisted living facility that specialized in dementia.

This decision helped Henry to steady his life. Like Henry, you may **take steps to steady your life**. List possible steps on paper, choose one, and start working on it. You may accept a different job within your company, for example, or work fewer hours. Acting in your own behalf will make you feel better and more in control of things. Slowly, you work your way through early grief.

Find activities to take your mind off grief. Robert Veniga, MD, author of *A Gift of Hope: How We Survive Our Tragedies*, calls these activities mental workouts. He thinks most of us know we need to exercise our bodies, but are less of aware of exercising our minds. "Hobbies are often forgotten," he writes. "In fact, we may even feel guilty about enjoying them."

Choose activities that are meaningful to you. Perhaps you're interested in photography. You could photograph buildings in your community, take close-ups of flowers, or portraits of family members. These activities are more than distractions, they are emotionally satisfying, and you need that right now.

SMILING THROUGH YOUR TEARS: ANTICIPATING GRIEF

Emotional Limbo

Early grief may intensify, plateau, and intensify again. That's because you're in emotional limbo. John S. Stephenson, PhD, in the book *Death & Identity,* says emotional limbo comes with the early grief territory. "The individual is in a state of emotional limbo, unable to resolve the loss because it has not yet occurred," he writes, "and at the same time, unable to avoid the authoritative diagnosis that death will occur."

What is emotional limbo? It's an emotional state that produces confusing feelings. Family members and friends may be baffled by your feelings. No doubt about it, emotional limbo is painful territory. You don't know what to expect from day to day. **Recognize your emotional limbo** and allow yourself to fluctuate, but don't be surprised if friends and family misunderstand your behavior. To them you are a different person, almost a stranger, and that's unsettling.

As you continue your early grief journey, try to **identify and talk about your feelings.** Bottling up your feelings isn't as beneficial as talking about them. You may be the kind of person who prefers to talk with a professionally trained therapist or physician. Other options include talking with clergy, a trusted friend, and joining a support group. The bottom line: let our feelings out.

The Time Factor

Early grief is almost worse than post-death grief because you don't know when death will come. Distant relatives and friends, people you thought you could rely on, may not expect you to feel distress. Why are you grieving if no one has died? Some family members may become short-tempered with you, while others may accuse you of "borrowing trouble."

Neither is true. You're going through early grief. Watching the decline of someone you love and care about is one of life's most painful experiences. How much time does your loved one have left? How much time can you spend with this person? Are there other demands on your time? Is your life slipping away? Will your life ever return to normal?

The time factor can grind you down. Instead of worrying about time, a better course of action is to **make the most of the time you have**. Here are some suggestions.

- Create new joyous memories with your loved one: family get-togethers, picnics, and holiday celebrations.
- Nurture other relationships in your life.
- Take the time to reflect and relax.
- Appreciate nature, such as a walk in the park to observe the changing seasons and wildlife.

Helpful as these actions may be, they can't shield you from the suspense and fear of early grief. Fear can take over your life, according to Dr. Robert Veniga. He says the victims of tragedy often believe things will only get worse, not better. "Their lives are governed by fears—a fear that they might not be strong enough to survive the crisis," he writes. "Perhaps a fear they can never again find happiness." You may feel this way.

Suspense and Fear

Suspense and fear also make early grief unique. Susan Duke writes about these feelings in her article, "An Exploration of Anticipatory Grief: the Lived Experience of People During Their Spouses' Terminal Illness and in Bereavement." Duke cites some of the themes related to suspense and fear.

- Keeping feelings inside
- Constant feeling of uncertainty

SMILING THROUGH YOUR TEARS: ANTICIPATING GRIEF

- Feeling like you're living in a time warp
- Emotional overload (You don't think you can take any more.)
- Being in crisis
- Walking a tightrope

Fear and suspense are emotional weights. Nobody is immune from these feelings, not even a United States Senator. In a letter to the newspaper Senator Rod Grams of Minnesota described his fear in simple, eloquent words. For years his 21-year old son has struggled with drug addiction, disappearing several times, and serving time in jail. These actions weigh heavily on Grams.

"Every time my telephone rings, my heart stops for a moment," he says, "for I live with the fear . . . that my son's addiction has cost my child his life." Grams' prayer is that no other family will have to go through a similar experience.

Fear may be directly connected to the person you're grieving for, as with Senator Grams' fear for his son, or connected to other life events. **Recognize suspense and fear** and give yourself credit for tying to handle them. If you had to handle suspense and fear alone you could probably do it, but you're already handling too much. Plus, early grief keeps getting more complex.

Complexity of Early Grief

Some grief experts believe early grief is more complex than post-death grief. Why? Therese A. Rando, PhD tells why in her article, "Anticipatory Grief: The Term is a Misnomer but the Phenomenon Exists." She says early grief imposes many limits on your life. Special events, such as birthday parties, anniversaries, graduations, and family reunions, stimulate your grief. Your early grief is always expanding due to losses yet to come.

In her book, *Loss & Anticipatory Grief,* Rando looks at the complexity of early grief again. "It is absolutely critical to recognize that a major component of early grief is the mourning of the absence of a loved one in the future." This void is the root of your pain. For your loved one's death will leave a huge void in your life. If your partner is terminally ill you face many losses: companionship, humor, mental stimulation, emotional support, help with chores, and loss of a sexual partner.

Each loss is an emotional wound.

While most people expect you to feel "normal" grief, they may not understand early grief at all. Early grief is outside their life experience. Stop and think for a minute. **Figure out what makes your early grief complex.** Are there many factors or just a few? Can you change any of the factors? If you can't change them, can you minimize them?

Knowing about early grief's complexity will help you to process it. Once you have this understanding you may be easier on yourself. You may even allow yourself to hope. To quote Harriet Goldhor Lerner, PhD, "As long as you feel hope, there is hope." A tiny spark of hope may keep you going.

Hope

Hope is probably the most unique feature of early grief. John S. Stephenson, PhD, a contributing writer for *Death & Identity,* writes about hope and its affect. "When the person's physical status is diagnosed as 'terminal' those involved with the patient may experience the shock of impending loss and yet be tempered with hope." Tempered is a word choice that implies balance.

Often hope is hidden from view and you must search for it. Ginny found hope in the intensive care waiting room of a hospital. Though the room was filled with people it was totally silent, each occupant lost in his or her thoughts. Ginny flipped nervously through a magazine while she waited for news of her severely injured son.

Suddenly a man walked into the room. He had a smile on his face and a jaunty tweed hat on his head. Starting at one corner of the room, he went from person to person, and told his story. "I'm a computer programmer from Seattle," he began. "A few weeks ago I noticed I was having memory problems. I couldn't track or process numbers—not good for a man with my job."

During a check-up at a major medical center physicians found a tumor in the man's brain. The tumor was removed. "This hat covers my shaved head and my incision," he explained with a smile. "A few days ago I came here thinking I would die. Today I'm going home and I plan to return to work. So don't lose hope." He told his story over and over again.

Everyone in the room was touched by the inspiring story. After the man left they sat up straighter, made eye contact, and started talking with each other. The stranger's story and kindness had infused them with energy. Maybe, just maybe, things would turn out all right. Look for hope in your life. You need hope in order to complete your early grief journey and face its endpoint—death.

Endpoint

Post-death grief may go on indefinitely, whereas early grief ends with the death of the ill person. At this point early grief becomes post-death grief, a process of its own. Waiting for the endpoint is one of the hardest things you will ever do. Even harder, you don't know when the endpoint will come and so you're always anxious and on alert. You need to **prepare for the endpoint** for it will come.

"I'm tired of waiting for my mother to die," admitted a stressed daughter. "This sounds awful, I know, but I've been waiting for years, and I'm worn out. I can hardly make myself visit her." We can understand the daughter's early grief and the exhaustion that comes with it. Before we go on, let's stop for a minute and take a last look at the uniqueness of early grief.

What Makes Early Grief Unique?

- Focuses of past, present and future
- Uncompleted loss
- Emotional limbo
- Time factor, which is exhausting
- Ongoing suspense and fear
- Complexity (It may be more complex than post-death grief.)
- Feeling of sorrow tempered with hope
- The endpoint of death

You may view these factors as markers in your grief journey. As prepared as you think you are, early grief comes as a shock. Shock can literally stop you in your tracks. How can something you know about be a shock? It's a puzzling question. The most puzzling question of all: How am I going to get through this?

Shock of Early Grief

Edward Myers discusses the shock factor in his book, *When Parents Die: A Guide for Adults.* Though prolonged illness doesn't have the shock value of sudden death, Myers thinks it exacts a terrible toll on individuals and families. "If sudden death hits like an explosion, knocking you flat, then a slow decline arrives like a glacier, massive, unstoppable, grinding you down."

SMILING THROUGH YOUR TEARS: ANTICIPATING GRIEF

The grinding gets to you. You don't know when your loved one will die, therefore it's hard to plan family events, make career plans, or funeral arrangements. Life is topsy-turvy. Still, you may be able to strike a balance. Set aside time to think about your feelings and find opportunities to interact with family and friends. Remember that children grieve, too, and you need to help them.

Grieving Children

You may be so overcome with early grief that you miss the extent of your children's grief. What are they thinking? Even if you know your children well, you don't know all of their thoughts, and don't want to put ideas into the heads. Every morning you awaken to the same challenge—to protect and care for your children while you're in terrible emotional pain.

Mary McIver talks about this parenting challenge in her article, "Healing the Hurt." She says our children [and grandchildren] need us most "just at a time when we may have the least to give." One solution, according to McIver, is to be open with our kids and let them see our tears. We may also give them permission to grieve—an approach that may open an emotional dam.

If you're a parent, grandparent, relative, or concerned friend, find ways to help grieving children. Helping them will make *you* feel better. Young children don't have the same needs as older children, so use age-appropriate language. Don't cover too much at once. Here are some things you could say and do.

1. Remind children that they are deeply loved.
2. Encourage them to talk about their sad feelings and grief. This may also be played out with toys or depicted in drawings.
3. Stick to soothing, predictable routines.

4. Provide occasional treats (special activities or foods).
5. Encourage children to spend time with their friends and playmates.
6. Give them time to themselves to think or cry, but make it clear that you're available to talk.

Children—even babies—are intuitive and know if you're upset and trying to hide your feelings. Draw courage from your children's energy and spirit. With their welfare at heart, as well as your own, you may want to get some support. You don't have to go through early grief alone.

Support

With sudden death there is no chance to get help until after the event. But with early grief there is still time to get help. Take advantage of this time. The need for support is a reflection of the changing intensity of your grief. Just a few visits with a medical professional can give you the strength you need. Be sure to get support from trained and reliable people.

A mother whose son had AIDS found support readily after she became active in HIV and AIDS groups. Other family members reached out to her. They understood her emotional pain, which was intensified by the stigma of this particular disease. (Chapter seven, "When Early Grief Gets Complicated," contains more information on the stigma of disease.)

One size doesn't fit all when it comes to support. Research the kinds of support that are available to you. Over time, you may shift from one type of support to another, depending on your needs, and the needs of your family. More important than the type of support you get is your promise to **get some support**. Don't tough it out alone month after month.

You're vulnerable now and it's easy to be taken in by

quackery. "My husband didn't want to have a bone marrow transplant and he was willing to try anything," recalled a concerned wife. "He drank carrot juice until he turned orange. He ate totally raw food. He tried coffee enemas. I put charcoal poultices on his neck." After hearing her story we have a word of caution for you.

Be wary of unusual remedies like these. Also be wary of people who claim to have a secret formula, magic pills and ointments, give you unsolicited testimonials, try to sell you things on the phone, hound you, or use scare tactics. Before you try any odd remedies or medications talk with a physician.

A specialized facility, such as hospice care, may be just the kind of support you need. In his article, "Hospice: A Return to Old Ways," journalist John Weiss points out that hospice care may be in-home care. "Hospice care is the renewal of a way of life for people who are dying," he says.

In a related article Weiss says this is what hospice is all about. A daughter who was interviewed for the article describes her mother's death in hospice as a "wonderful death." You want to maintain your loved one's quality of life as long as possible. So investigate your options and determine which are best for you. You'll find hospice information on the Internet.

Different Opinions

Early grief is a controversial idea. Some researchers think it's just partial grief. Other researchers think it's "normal" grief that started early. Still others think early grief is a form of depression. A few researchers think early grief is marked hostility, a view that may offend you and your family. Who is right? The answer may depend on your experience.

Dr. Robert Buckman, author of *"I Don't Know What to Say:" How to Help and Support Someone Who is Dying*, sees early grief differently. Early grief isn't hostility or "a thought fathered by a wish to see the person dead," he writes. "We grieve before death just as we flinch when we anticipate being injured." Buckman's view may make you think of childhood experiences, such as flinching before you received a shot. You are flinching now because you know pain will come.

The debate on early grief continues. In their paper, "The Social Reconstruction of Anticipatory Grief," Graham Fulton and his colleagues state that early grief research is flawed. They believe early grief is a forewarning of loss—a response to the loss of meaning associated with a person. But word arguments don't necessarily apply to human emotions and the anecdotal evidence on early grief is mounting.

Early grief is an experience shared by people around the world. Because of terrorism, bioterrorism, suicide attacks, fragmented families, and the complexity of modern life, early grief seems to be increasing. Most of us can find examples of early grief in our lives.

The fact that early grief varies so much makes it a challenging concept. Early grief varies from week to week, varies in duration, and varies because your future is unclear. Alla Bozarth-Campbell, PhD talks about the confusion of early grief in his book, *Life is Goodbye, Life is Hello: Grieving Well Through All Kinds of Loss*. "There is an unspoken expectation that, while physical illness can't be helped, you are responsible for your emotional health and can control it at will," he writes. "This is simply not true."

Chances are you're reading this book because you know this isn't true. You're the one who is juggling the focuses, symptoms, affects, and emotions of early grief. Nobody can do it for you, not even brilliant, dedicated researchers with good intentions. Making sense of your emotions will take some time. Again, we have a word of caution here. Controlling your emotions is not the healthiest approach to take.

A healthier approach is to reflect on your feelings and let yourself feel them, even if they're painful. This allows you to resolve painful feelings and, over time, regain some serenity. At the very least, you get your life moving forward again.

Now you know what makes early grief unique. Unfortunately, the process is still poorly understood and poorly accepted. Those who are going through early grief often get less support and struggle alone—something else to grieve about. While early grief is a struggle, you aren't alone, and may find support in these healing steps.

Healing Steps

- Be aware of the focuses of early grief.
- Accept the fact that there is no way around grief.
- Take steps to steady your life.
- Find activities to take your mind off grief.
- Recognize your emotional limbo.
- Identify and talk about your feelings.
- Make the most of the time you have.
- Recognize your suspense and fear.
- Figure out what makes your early grief complex.
- Look for hope in your life.
- Prepare for early grief's endpoint.
- Help grieving children.
- Get some support.

CHAPTER 2
The Early Grief of Terrorism

When written in Chinese the word crisis is composed of two characters -
one represents danger and the other represents opportunity.

President John F. Kennedy

SMILING THROUGH YOUR TEARS: ANTICIPATING GRIEF

The early grief of terrorism is a new feeling for most Americans. We grieve for those who lost their lives on September 11th and for other losses as well: loss of security, loss of trust, loss of control, loss of life as we knew it, loss of concentration, and for some, the loss of purpose. You may attribute your anxious feelings to news reports when they're really early grief.

As you recall, early grief is a feeling of loss before a death or dreaded event occurs. The grief associated with terrorism has the same characteristics as early grief, with one exception. Early grief has an endpoint—death—whereas the early grief associated with terrorism has no endpoint; at least none is in sight. So we must prepare ourselves for the long haul.

Suicide attacks are killing people around the world and we see the television footage of the attacks within minutes. The footage is played over and over again and these images of death and destruction are stored in our minds. Indeed, these images have changed minds. To understand the early grief of terrorism you need to understand the power of September 11th. What made the attacks so devastating?

Power of September 11th

Trauma is the one-word answer to this question. Alan D. Wolfeldt, PhD, looks at trauma in his article, "A Nation Mourns: Understanding the Personal Symptoms of Trauma." According to Wolfeldt, the attacks of September 11th took away our sense of invulnerability and the notion of a predictable, orderly world. In other words, life is beyond our control.

"This tragedy taught us that we cannot fully control our

futures," he says. "We feel vulnerable, helpless and powerless." These are awful feelings and we wish they would go away and leave us alone. We wish for a simpler, more innocent time, when people didn't lock their houses or car doors or worry about terrorists in the community. In addition to making us feel vulnerable, the events of September 11th were devastating for other reasons.

- The element of surprise
- Our altered concept of reality
- Sheer brutality of the attacks
- Mass casualties and death
- Seeing the successful and failed rescue attempts
- Increased fear of terrorism
- Fear for our children's safety
- Anger at the US being a target
- Confusion as to why these people hate us so much
- Questions about our national security
- Impact on the national economy
- Impact on your local economy
- Anxious feelings and the need to stay close to home
- Our altered sense of freedom
- Loss of freedoms that we took for granted

The tragedies in New York City, Pennsylvania, and Washington, DC have become part of our history, and each of us must decide how we are going to respond to this history. Many have chosen to stay calm. In fact, the National Association of School Psychologists tells parents to **model calm behavior for children.** How can you do this?

Kids take their cues from parents [and grandparents], according to the association, and our calm approach is reassuring to them. Let the experts deal with terrorism—that's not our primary responsibility. Our responsibility is to take care of our children and us. That's enough responsibility for now.

Joy Amidst Grief

Kim Ode writes for the *Star-Tribune* in Minneapolis, MN and a recent column focuses on the tragic death of Darrel Lee Miller, husband of Laurie. Laurie and Darrell married, had four years together, and were blessed with a son. Then Darrel was diagnosed with cancer and, within a year, he was gone. The article said Laurie had to resist the impulse to mourn during his illness, which is early grief.

"We had to find even a kernel of joy in every day," Laurie told the *Star-Tribune*.

The early grief of terrorism comes into our lives like an unexpected houseguest standing on the doorstep with too much baggage and intentions of staying a while. Though life has forced us to let this "guest" in the door, we can resist the impulse to give in to the early grief of terrorism. Like Darrell and Laurie Miller, you may look for **look for life's kernels of joy.** It may take a while for you to recognize these kernels, but if you look closely and constantly, you will see them everywhere.

Shift from Present to Future

The early grief of terrorism shifts our attention from the present to the future. Will the terrorists attack us again? When will they strike? Where will they strike? Terrorism makes us fear death like we've never feared it before. Death is our deepest, most chilling fear, not the death of one person, but the death of thousands. We grieve for the world and worry about the kind of world our children and grandchildren will inherit.

Reports of war casualties also make us fear death. A newspaper article, "Wed in a Week," tells how John Heaser and Christina Snow wed quickly because he received military orders. "With me leaving, I wanted her to know that my love is for life," the groom said, adding that he didn't know when he would see his bride again. His unspoken question: Will I *ever* see her again?

Fear is the terrorist's goal. The terrorists want to paralyze us with fear, to cripple us financially and emotionally. We don't have to give terrorists this victory. Instead, we can be alert to our shifts in focus and **focus on the present.** As the poet Carl Sandburg once wrote, "The past is a bucket of ashes, so live not in your yesterdays, nor just for tomorrow, but in the here and now."

Confronting Terrorism

Terrorists planned the events September 11th in detail, trained for them, and waited years to strike. If they succeeded once they may succeed again. That's why we must **confront terrorism** with everything we have like Israel. Israel has a security plan and a terrorism response plan. Minutes after a terrorist attack, police, medical, and clean-up teams are on the scene.

The wounded are treated, the dead are respectfully removed, and clean up begins. Crews work at a frantic pace, sweeping up broken glass, removing bloodstains from walls, hauling burned cars away, putting up new walls and windows, and restocking shelves. By the next day virtually all evidence of terrorism is gone. What's the message?

Israel is telling the terrorists—and the world—that terrorism and suicide attacks will not prevail.

And so, despite profound sorrow and fear, the Israelis go

about their daily lives. In 1991 the renowned violinist Itzak Pearlman was giving a concert in Tel Aviv when the terror alert sirens sounded. "Everyone had brought their gas masks with them and we put them on quickly," recalled an audience member. "Itzak Pearlman didn't put on a gas mask or miss a beat. He kept right on playing."

She went on to say that she thought about the evening often and wondered how the audience looked from Pearlman's vantage point. "The gas masks have large tubes on the front," she said. "We must have looked like hundreds of elephants sitting together. I don't know how he kept playing with the sirens sounding. You would think he would lose his place in the music, but he didn't."

Like Pearlman, you may continue to play your life concert. You may balance the early grief of terrorism with the fact that you're alive—a blessing in itself. Life is a miracle. Hold this thought in your mind and bring it forth when the day seems long and you're discouraged. It will help you cope with crisis, a terrible burden for anyone.

Burden of Crisis

Seeing the television pictures of Ground Zero made Americans cry and people around the world cried with us. Certainly, the sight stunned those who visited the cavernous hole, even Red Cross workers like Kristin. The Red Cross sent Kristin, a grief counselor, to New York City to help victims' families. Her task was to help family members come to terms with the attack and begin the healing process.

Each day, Kristin took groups of 80-100 people, including firefighters' families, to Ground Zero. The scene had such an impact on Kristin that she was forced to turn away from it. "I wouldn't have been able to speak to the family members if I was looking at Ground Zero," she said.

Terrorism and grief are a heavy burden and you may wish to get crisis counseling. You'll find help on the Internet by using the search words *terrorism* and *response*. Before you sign up for anything, however, find out about the organization. Your physician should also be able to refer you to a trained crisis counselor.

Scope of Grief

Terrorism has cast a dark shadow over the world. When you think about terrorism you may also think about global terrorism, bioterrorism, weapons of mass destruction, and warfare. All of these topics are terrifying. News reports and terror alerts may change the intensity of your grief. It's not fun to have your emotions bouncing around like a rubber ball.

The early grief of terrorism is so broad that your support system may not be able to keep pace with it. Whether it's conscious or unconscious, you may find yourself using your support system differently. "We used to go to church for spiritual comfort and now all we hear is political wrangling," a couple explained. "We feel very alone." The arguments upset the couple so much that they became selective about their church attendance. They checked the church newsletter regularly and, if the sermon sounded controversial, stayed home. On the other hand, if the sermon sounded uplifting they went to church.

Perhaps all they needed was to **talk about terrorism.** Stanley Cornils, author of *The Mourning After: How to Manage Grief Wisely*, thinks conversation is an emotional release. "Each time we talk about a painful experience, our pain is eased just a little bit more," he writes. His advice sounds good, but how do you start a conversation about terrorism?

You may start with a question: "Did you see the television

special on terrorism last night?" You may start with a request: "Are you having as much trouble with this terrorism stuff as I am?" You may start with an idea: "Maybe we should start a terrorism support group." The seed of an idea can grow into a sturdy means of support.

Talking With Kids

Somehow, we must find a way to work through our emotions while helping kids work through theirs. Can we do it? Yes, because we must. Kids are smart and talk about scary things when they think you're not listening and when you're not around. But kids' fears can magnify quickly and you don't want that to happen. **Talk with kids about terrorism.**

- Tell kids the truth—terrorists attacked our country.
- Admit you're upset. (You don't have to go into this in detail.)
- Tell kids it's OK for them to be upset.
- Assure kids that they're safe.
- Stick to the facts.
- Keep it short.
- Use age-appropriate words.
- Listen carefully to their responses.
- Watch body language.
- Show your love and support.

Teens react differently to terrorism than youngsters and may make outrageous comments. In the article, "The Clinical Lessons of 9/11," psychology professor Martha B. Strauss tells about one teen's reaction to seeing the Twin Towers fall. "It happened, it sucked, and it ruined a lot of lives," said the 14-year-old girl. "Get over it."

Flip comments like these often mask deep emotion. Remember, preteen and teen behavior can change in minutes.

An hour from now teens may be munching pizza and joking with friends. Nevertheless, teens may still be worried about terrorism, so be patient and observant. Watch for signs of depression and get professional help for teens if you think they need it.

Coping With Suspense and Fear

After September 11th many local families were afraid, according to Kristin, the Red Cross grief counselor. "Families were terrified and they still are," she said. Some New Yorkers vowed never to take the subway again. Others packed up and moved away. And others were so fearful they didn't know what to do. Thank goodness there are steps we can take to cope with suspense and fear.

1. **Pay attention to your children's health.** Stress can take a toll on children, according to the National Association of School Psychologists. Whether you're the parent of teens, grade-schoolers, or preschoolers, make sure your kids eat a balanced diet, exercise regularly, and get enough sleep. Try to eat at least one meal together each day.

2. **Get to know your community resources.** Find the nearest hospital, fire station, and police station. Put a list of emergency phone numbers by the phone. Figure out how long it takes to get to these places. Contact your kids' school and ask about support groups and counseling. Local agencies may also offer workshops on responding to terrorism.

3. **Encourage youngsters to express their feelings through art.** Keep art materials, such as watercolor markers, on hand. Hang some of the pictures on the refrigerator door. Talk about the drawings with your kids. Call your local art center, if you have one, and ask about art classes for children.

4. **Limit television viewing.** In the age of 24-hour news

coverage many stories are repeats, and you don't have to see them all. Young children should NOT see news coverage of terrorism. Turn off the set and get them involved in something else. Take the time to play games with your kids or go for a walk together.

5. Replace your negative thoughts with positive ones. For example, you may focus on the courage and dedication of local firefighters. Write the chief and thank him and the firefighters for all that they do. Go to the library and checkout resources on firefighters, policemen and policewomen, and other community workers.

6. Stay in contact with family members. If there ever was a time to stick close to your kids, resolve family arguments, and link the generations, this is it. Get together for a family picnic or potluck supper. To prevent needless worry, keep family members apprised of your plans: dates, times, places, contact names, and phone numbers. Update family members regularly.

Getting Through It

Rony Berger, PhD, Director of Community Services at the Trauma Center for Victims of Terror and War in Israel, saw the plane crash into the World Trade Center building on television. "Suddenly it felt as if there was no safe place on earth," he writes. Working with trauma victims taught Berger an important lesson.

Instead of counseling people right away Berger takes on a "holder" role for trauma victims and acts like a container for their experience. Berger holds people, listens to them, and comforts them. Only later, when he feels the survivors are ready, does he counsel them. We may learn from Berger's experience.

Give yourself some time to adjust to the early grief of terrorism. **Learn about terrorism** during this time. This isn't fun learning, to be sure, but it's necessary. Just as the terrorists studied us, so we must study them. Check government Web sites for information on travel restrictions. Bookstores carry books about terrorism and you'll find others listed in *Books in Print*, an online publication.

We will get through these times together. While we don't know all of the terrorists, we know many. We don't know all of their methods, but we're learning about them. Though we can't protect every person every moment, security measures are in place and they're working. In short, our nation is getting smarter and we need to do the same. Planning ahead is one way to do this.

Plan Ahead

Michael Osterholm, PhD, MPH, Director of the Center for Infectious Diseases at the University of Minnesota, is an expert on bioterrorism. In a speech to the Minnesota Medical Association Alliance, Osterholm said Americans enjoy a good, busy lifestyle, "but my greatest fear is that we get so busy we forget September 11th. We must never, ever forget!"

Osterholm thinks every family, including his own, should **make a terrorism plan.** The plan will help you regain control over your life and help you to handle the early grief of terrorism. Having a terrorism plan also saves time. Your plan should cover these key points, according to Osterholm.

- Determine a central meeting place—a place family members can get to easily. You may also wish to have an alternate destination, such as a family cabin.

- Have redundant systems, such as multiple phone lines and several cell phones. Keep your cell phones charged.
- Make sure that your systems aren't all in one place. In other words, have a back-up plan or plans.
- Give every family member a copy of the plan. Put your plan in writing and distribute it to family members.

Older kids may find comfort in working out the details of the plan with you, such as assembling a first-aid kit. The American Red Cross has developed the "Facing the Fear" program to help young people deal with terrorism and tragic events. Contact your local Red Cross chapter or access www.redcross.org for more information on this interactive program.

Terrorism may not end in our lifetime, yet we must remain hopeful. How can we do this? Mayo Clinic psychiatrist Sheila Jowsey, MD thinks we need to "**move from hopelessness to helpfulness.**" We do this by focusing on available resources and staying current on safety information. The early grief of terrorism gives us the opportunity to cherish our families, our friends, and our lives. Take advantage of this opportunity.

Healing Steps

- Understand the power of September 11th.
- Model calm behavior for children.
- Look for life's kernels of joy.
- Focus on the present.
- Confront terrorism.
- Get crisis counseling if you think you need it.
- Talk about terrorism.
- Talk with kids about terrorism.

- Get to know your community resources.
- Encourage kids to express their feelings with art.
- Limit television viewing.
- Replace negative thoughts with positive ones.
- Stay in contact with family members.
- Learn about terrorism.
- Make a terrorism plan.
- Move from hopelessness to helpfulness.

CHAPTER 3
Grief As a Reaction to Change

Where there is sorrow, there is holy ground.

Oscar Wilde

SMILING THROUGH YOUR TEARS: ANTICIPATING GRIEF

Take away emotion from grief and you are left with a reaction to change. The health of your loved one or friend has changed for the worse. It's frightening. Grief expert Elizabeth Kubler-Ross thinks the fear of death is universal and says we fear it "even if we think we have mastered it on many levels." Early grief is as frightening as post-death grief.

Your fears may be fueled by the inexactness of grief. Jo-Eileen Gyulay, RN, PhD, in her article "Grief Responses," describes post-death grief as a blurred and muddy journey. Early grief is also blurred and muddy journey and our acceptance of it doesn't come easily. Some of us fight acceptance every step of the way. The only way to find acceptance, Gyulay says, is to experience the pain of loss.

Early grief is filled with change. Despite intense emotional pain, you may find the strength to go on, yet feel like you're always a step behind. Life feels like a constant game of catch-up; one misstep and you could fall. The going gets harder because life is changing so fast. What kinds of changes are you facing?

Changes in Your Place

Alla Bozarth-Campbell, PhD, author of *Life is Goodbye, Life is Hello*, thinks the basic changes of life are place, position, and person. **Become aware of these changes.** This requires effort and observation, but your efforts will help you to adjust. These efforts may also lead to solutions.

A change in place refers to your home and community—your space. While your home and community may not be perfect, they are familiar to you. This is comforting. Even if you have just moved to a new community it may feel right. "You know how you feel in your own space," says Bozarth-Campbell. "Life is secure."

But some people must relocate in order to get the medical care they need. Perhaps you had to move your parent into a nursing home, or your family to a community that has a large medical center. Personal health problems may force you to move into an assisted living facility. You don't want to do this, but know you must.

The life that was secure now feels insecure.

Without familiar faces and surroundings you may feel lost. Though you were a confident person in the past you may not feel confident now. How can you feel better? **Take steps to feel more secure.** Finding a new friend to walk with may ingrain a familiar routine and provide new social connections. Church suppers, neighborhood groups, and special clubs (bridge, quilting, book, etc.) also provide new social contacts.

While new social contacts may ease early grief, they don't erase it, or the changes in your life. We cause many of these changes ourselves, while others come as a complete surprise, or even a shock. You may confront *all* of life's basic changes in the midst of early grief. That's what happened to Lillian. (Remember her name because Lillian's story comes up again later.)

The first change came when her husband was diagnosed with an aggressive form of cancer. She quit her job so she could be home with him. Lack of a second income and mounting medical bills forced the couple to sell their home and most of their furniture. To further economize and have a sitter for their young son, the couple moved in with Lillian's mother. All of these decisions—quitting her job, selling her home, moving in with a parent—changed her place in life. "I lost everything, my job, my home, my furniture, and my neighborhood," she said.

Lillian relied on her mother's support all though her husband's chemotherapy, relapse, recurrence of disease, more chemotherapy, and countless trips to the emergency room. Then her mother had a severe asthma attack in the middle of the night, and was rushed to the hospital by ambulance. Two days later her mother died of a heart attack.

"I couldn't believe it,' Lillian said. "I couldn't believe my mother died before my husband. I was in total shock." As is normal with post-death grief, she became angry at her mother for deserting her at such a stressful time. But Lillian didn't have the time to waste on anger because she was forced to deal with other issues.

An aunt had died several months before her mother died. Two successive deaths in the family had changed its structure. Family members were so overcome with grief they couldn't help Lillian. To make matters worse, some family members accused her of hastening her mother's death by moving into the house. Lillian didn't believe this.

"I knew my Mom and knew that she was less stressed helping us than she would have been watching us," she explained. "It was better for her to do that for me." In hindsight, Lillian realized her mother's asthma was far worse than she thought. Then too, her mother may have hidden the seriousness of her condition from her daughter.

The death of her mother left an empty space in Lillian's life. She had gotten used to her mother's support and now that support was gone. Lillian would pick up the phone to call her mother, only to remember that she had died. "I could hardly believe it," she said. "I had some almost anxiety attacks because I was out there by myself."

Lillian, her husband and son continued to live in her mother's house. But family members wanted them to vacate the premises and transfer her husband to a nursing home so the estate could be settled. Determined to be strong for her husband, her son, and herself, Lillian refused to move. It wasn't long, though, before her husband needed hospice care.

A few months later, after a six-year battle with cancer, her husband died. His death changed Lillian's position in life. Now she was a widow, on her own, and solely responsible for her son's welfare. On the first anniversary of her husband's death she was able to see her life more clearly. It was a life totally shattered by change.

Changes in Your Position

Like Lillian, you may still be adjusting to one change when another comes into your life. Changes in position are stressful because they are woven into your identity. If you have been through changes in position, such as a job transfer, switching from full-time to part-time, or getting "downsized," you understand the stress involved.

While you are adjusting to life's changes you are also adjusting to the changes of early grief.

Changes in your position don't negate your intelligence, talents, or training—they're still part of you. However, changes in position may lead to some painful questions. You may question your parenting, your occupation, your likes and dislikes, where you live, the car you drive, your goals in life and plans for achieving them. "I questioned everything," Lillian said. "Everything was up for grabs."

In the midst of such chaos you need to **set aside time for reflection.** Quiet times often lead to surprising discoveries and you may discover a new self. Your discoveries may result in a different home or apartment, different job, and different community. Setting aside time for reflection may draw you closer to those you love. What a blessing.

Changes in Your Person

Person is the third basic life change and includes marriage, parenthood, promotion, divorce, and retirement. It also includes your appearance, which may change rapidly or gradually. If you have been grieving a long time you may look so different that people barely recognize you. Indeed, you may hardly recognize yourself.

Mary was in her early fifties when her father developed severe emphysema due to decades of smoking. His emphysema became so bad that he moved into a nursing home, where he subsequently died. The shock of his death caused her mother to have a stroke. Meanwhile, both of her children developed serious health problems and, though they survived, it took years for them to recover.

Ongoing crisis changed Mary's appearance. Photos taken during this time show an exhausted, depressed, and rapidly aging woman. After this time of crisis had passed, however, Mary began to look like herself again. Her eyes sparkled and she smiled more often and was excited about life. Some friends thought she looked younger than her age.

Changes in person are especially painful. Your loved one may have hair loss due to chemotherapy, a moon face due to steroids, hemiplegia (paralysis) due to stroke, profound height and weight loss, or be curled in a fetal position. "Something grievous has interrupted our lives and shaken us, slightly or greatly, from our sureness about ourselves," says Bozarth-Campbell. "The very sense of self may be dimmed, dulled, or deadened."

Changes in place, position, and person may change you. To get a snapshot of what you have been through, **add up the changes.** Fold a piece of paper into thirds for person, position, and place. List the changes under each category. Which category has the most listings? Which changes were the most painful? Put a check mark by the recent changes, such as the declining health of a pet.

Changes in Your Pet

Pets are often substitute children for couples who have no kids of their own. Anticipating the death of a pet can be as traumatic for these couples as anticipating the death of a person. They are about to lose a member of the family, and the family unit will never be the same. Watching her cat die slowly from liver cancer devastated one professional woman.

"I didn't have any children so my cat was my child," she said. "When he died I was so upset I took a day off from work. My boss understood my grief and came to visit me. I thought that was really kind." Several months later her cat's photo was featured on the cover of a pet magazine. Though she was still grieving for her cat, seeing his picture brought back happy memories. "I thought it was a good tribute," she said with tears in her eyes.

Journalists Cokie and Steve Roberts talk about caring for a dying pet in their article, "Puppy Love: the Final Days of a Bedraggled and Beloved Old Basset Hound." The dog's name was Abner and, as his illness progressed, he needed to be carried and lost control of body functions. Still, the Roberts viewed caring for their dying pet as a blessing. Abner loved them unconditionally and they loved him the same way.

"How many things in life are that plain and pure?" they ask. Surely their positive attitude helped the Roberts get through early and post-death grief. **Adjusting your attitude** can help you to heal. It's hard to find a positive attitude when you are overcome with early grief. Family members and friends may help you all they can, but adjusting your attitude is really up to you.

Measuring Early Grief

You may want to start out by examining your early grief. Ruth Huber, PhD and John W. Gibson, DSW describe a self-assessment tool in their study, "New Evidence for Early grief." To help people track their journey through early grief Huber devised something called "The 10-Mile Mourning Bridge."

Huber and Gibson surveyed 134 family members after their loved ones had died. The deceased had received hospice care and most of the family members had been caregivers. Sixty percent were wives or daughters. Huber came up with a visual analog based on the image of a bridge. It's a simple tool.

First, Huber drew a horizontal line. Then she put numbers on top of the line, starting with 0 on the left and ending with 10 on the right. Users pinpointed their location on the bridge at various times in their lives. When they reach 10 they had presumably completed their early grief. People who failed to grasp the bridge image were eliminated from Huber's study. Before the participants were given the self-assessment tool they were asked general questions about hospice care. They were asked specific questions regarding the bridge. One question: "How much (if any) of the 10-Mile Mourning Bridge had you already crossed by the time your loved one had died, due to hospice care?" The average response was 4.6 miles.

"In other words, the bereaved who responded felt that nearly half of their grief work had been accomplished through the work of the hospice team, prior to the actual occurrence of death," say the authors.

Interestingly, respondents who were more than 60 years old often saw themselves as being farther across the bridge at the time of their loved one's death than younger people. The reasons for this are unclear. Perhaps these people had more experience to draw upon. Older people may also be more accepting of death.

The researchers acknowledge the study's limitations. Because this was the first time the self-assessment tool was used there was no data on it. Participants may have given partial answers due to the highly emotional nature of grief. Some participants may have wanted to give "good" and "pleasing" answers. Lastly, this study is based on participants' memories, which may have been hazy.

Still, "The 10-Mile Mourning Bridge" may help you to see where you are in life. **Assess your own early grief.** Draw a line bridge, write the numbers on top, and mark your current location. Think about your first step on the bridge, subsequent steps, and how far you have to go.

Other early grief tests have been developed. They give you a clearer picture of where you have been and where you are headed. Helpful as these tests may be, they probably won't help you measure the early grief of terrorism, a new focus of study for researchers. Early grief is a recurring process with built-in changes that make you vulnerable.

Change Makes You Vulnerable

According to an old adage, the only thing that is constant in life is change. Like ocean waves rolling up on a beach, many changes may roll into your life. Low waves of change may swirl about your feet. Large waves of change may shift your balance. Huge waves of change may knock you down.

Extreme change, especially changes our own health, make

us vulnerable. NFL Hall-of-Fame member Walter Payton revealed his vulnerability at a press conference in February of 1999. Journalist Hank Gola describes the conference in his article, "Payton Awaits a Liver." After he told reporters that Mayo Clinic doctors had discovered he had a rare liver disease, Payton broke down and cried.

The disease, Primary Sclerosing Cholangitis, affects about three out of every 100,000 people and Payton was one of them. He said his name had been added to Mayo Clinic's transplant list. Payton handled the press conference well until reporters asked him if he had a message for friends. He asked people to pray for him and fell into his son's arms. Payton's actions suggest he was grieving for himself. You may be grieving for yourself, the medical diagnosis you received, the prospect of treatment, and life coming to a close.

Robert Fulton, in "The Many Faces of Grief," notes that patients may anticipate their own deaths. "They are often aware of the emotional undercurrents in an environment in which everyone is waiting for something to happen," he writes. Waiting is hard on everyone—patients, family members, and health professionals. You're always waiting for the other shoe to drop.

Dorothy Caruso-Herman, BSN writes about self-grief in her article, "Concerns for the Dying Patient and Family." Most patients are informed of their prognosis today, she says, and participate in their treatment decisions, including when to stop treatment. According to the researcher, health professionals need to incorporate an awareness of grief into all care plans. Her suggestion would help patients, family members, and health professionals.

Despite their illness, many terminally ill patients are able to accomplish things. Some have been inspired to become organ donors and encouraged others to do the same. Chapter nine, "How Early Grief May Help You," talks about making something productive out of grief. Has change made you feel vulnerable? Do you recognize these feelings? Can you live with them for a while? **Recognizing vulnerability** will help you take protective measures. For example, this may not be the time to buy a new car or make other major purchases. Focus on the changes you face now instead of creating new ones.

Change Alters Life

Life happens. We wish it would wait for us, but it doesn't, as Jeff discovered. Jeff was in his late fifties when his daughter was diagnosed with cancer. A health professional, Jeff knew that cancer treatments had improved greatly and believed his daughter would get well. Months passed and Jeff's emotional support of his daughter never wavered.

His daughter was on the road to recovery when Jeff, himself, was diagnosed with cancer. He had to make some crucial life decisions in a very short time. Within hours, Jeff changed from a caring parent to someone who needed care. This role reversal turns up often in the medical literature.

Susan Duke focuses on spousal caregivers in her study, "An exploration of Anticipatory Grief: the Lived Experience of People During Their Spouses' Terminal Illness and in Bereavement." Her small study of four participants makes some large points. Duke asked the participants to recall the time just before their spouse had died—the time of early grief. As the health of their loved ones declined the spouses changed from giving care to needing it. Interestingly, the study participants described the death of their spouses less vividly than their early grief feelings.

"I felt like my life had come to a stop," one said. "I knew

my husband was going to die but I didn't know how or when and I didn't know if I wanted to know these things."

Figure out how much you want to know. Your spouse may be scheduled for bypass heart surgery, for example. To conserve energy, you ask doctors for information on the procedure: what is involved, how long it takes, recovery time, and risk factors. You don't need to know every single detail because that gives you more to worry about. Spend your energy on emotional support for your spouse and taking care of yourself. Trust health professionals to do their jobs.

Medicine changes so rapidly that most doctors are reluctant to make predictions about life expectancy. Doctors, nurses, and experts may struggle to provide an accurate prediction for you. No matter what the timeline is, it will be difficult to believe and accept. Sometimes no clear answers are possible and that is the reality of change.

Accepting Reality

Alla Bozarth-Campbell, PhD, in his book, *Life is Goodbye, Life is Hello*, says news stories about natural disasters and inhuman cruelties make us hurt more. When we try to ignore these stories we are shutting out reality. We must **accept the reality of change**, something that's easier said than done.

Slowing down helped one wife to see reality more clearly. "I'm on the go all the time so I had to focus on slowing down," she said. "I had to pull back and let the pain come—let the grief come. It was really hard. It was really painful. But I knew I had to do it." Much to her surprise, life seemed a bit easier after she was willing to accept pain.

Family grief therapy has helped some people to accept the realities of change. David W. Kissane and his colleagues discuss this approach in their article, "Family Grief Therapy"

A Preliminary Account of a New Model to Promote Healthy Family Functioning During Palliative Care and Bereavement."

Many families are able to deal with grief, its resolution, and move on to a creative and productive life, the researchers say, but vulnerable families may need professional help. The researchers identified five types of families: supportive, conflict resolving, intermediate, sullen, and hostile. They invited members of the dying patient's immediate family, as well as the patient, to workshops led by trained therapists.

One goal of the workshops was to promote the sharing of grief. Kissane and his team worked to create an empathetic relationship with the dying person's family to help family members cope with their feelings. The researchers don't think these preventive measures should be applied only to families in need. Other families may benefit from this kind of help.

For more information on family grief therapy call your local hospital or hospice. Acceptance of reality comes at quiet times, when the television and radio are off, when you aren't talking, and when you are alone with yourself. During these times awful thoughts may enter your mind. You don't want to hear them, but you must, in order to move beyond early grief. This is raw pain.

Earl A. Grollman, an expert on grief and author of 26 books, believes pain is a universal tie that binds people together. In an article called "Coping With Loss: Teachings of a Master," he describes grief as nature's way of healing a broken heart. You may feel like your heart is broken right now and wonder if it will ever heal.

Though your acceptance wavers from one day to the next, early grief helps to heal a broken heart. At times you may retreat into denial. Once you accept your situation, however, you are better able to make decisions about the future. These decisions can help you to improve matters for yourself, your family, and others.

Health Professionals' Grief

Health professionals' grief is inter-related with that of family members. Alun Jones, RMN writes about nurses' grief in his article, "Actors in an Emotional Drama: Inter-related Grief in Terminal Care." Jones, who is a psychiatric nurse, thinks a patient's terminal illness creates a range of responses in nurses. The responses are an attempt to shield them from early grief.

"Caring for a person who is dying is one of the most distressing tasks nurses can undertake," he said. "The confrontation with death and the inevitable anxiety elicits defensive behaviors."

Jones observed nurses carefully and some acted as if the patient had not spoken. Some nurses changed the topic of conversation or adopted a "jokey atmosphere" to relieve tension. Nurses would become intensely involved with tasks. Occasionally, nurses would pretend to be needed elsewhere in the hospital.

Defensive behaviors such as these aren't limited to nurses. Doctors may shorten their visits to distance themselves from patients. Health professionals may also distract themselves and family members with tests of peripheral value. University of Minnesota Robert Fulton thinks health professionals may reverse roles with family members.

In his book, *The Many Faces of Grief,* Fulton says early grief may turn professional caregivers (doctors, nurses, nursing assistants, technicians, etc.) into surrogate grievers. "The caregiver grieves but is not bereaved," he explains, "while the bereft survivor may be beyond experiencing his or her grief."

The surrogate griever response may confuse you. Still, you may look upon health professionals' early grief as intense caring. Health professionals may be able to predict the timing and nature of death better than family members who are emotionally overwhelmed. Let's be respectful of early grief in others and in ourselves. Ground Zero is a sorrowful place for Americans, yet it is holy ground. Early grief is also a sorrowful place and may be considered holy ground. Keep this in mind while you're going through it. **Be understanding of health professionals' grief.** Like you, they are doing their best and that's all we can ask.

Coping With Change

Perhaps you have already lost loved ones, a beloved parent, grandparent, or aunt. Even if you have experienced loss before, this coming loss may feel different. Coping methods that worked before may not work now. Your hobbies may seem less interesting and your best friend, the one you always relied on, has moved away.

Life has changed so much you feel like you're lost in the fog. **Find new ways to cope with change.** Look at both the positive and negative aspects. If the negative aspects are more common, you will want to protect yourself for a while. Slow the pace, try to minimize change, and assess your status. Here are some more suggestions from people who have "been there."

- Trust your instincts. If something doesn't feel right, chances are it isn't.
- Strengthen your spiritual beliefs. You may learn more about them and/or place more trust in spirituality.
- Let people help you. Even if you are fiercely independent, accept help in this time of need.

- If family members are in too much pain to help you, get professional grief counseling.
- Get professional grief counseling for your child or children if you think it is necessary.
- Set new goals and visualize them. You may imagine yourself in a new apartment, for example, and decorate it in your mind.

You don't have to find new ways of coping right away. **Give yourself time to heal.** In this instance time *is* on your side. A new life is waiting, a life you make for yourself, and worthy of your best efforts. Go for it. Give yourself time to get your bearings and craft the contours of this life.

Healing Steps

- Be aware of life's basic changes: place, position, and person.
- Take steps to feel more secure.
- Set aside time for reflection.
- Add up the changes you have faced.
- Adjust your attitude.
- Assess your early grief.
- Recognize your vulnerability.
- Figure out how much you want to know.
- Accept the reality of change.
- Be understanding of health professionals' grief.
- Find new ways to cope with change.
- Give yourself time to heal.

CHAPTER 4
Factors That Shape Early Grief

*You gain strength, courage and confidence by every experience
in which you really stop and look fear in the face.
You are able to say to yourself, "I lived through this horror.
I can take the next thing that comes along."*

Eleanor Roosevelt

SMILING THROUGH YOUR TEARS: ANTICIPATING GRIEF

Personality is one of the main factors that shape early grief. The *Dictionary of Psychology* contains several definitions of personality. While experts disagree on some points, they agree that personality is an enduring pattern of traits. These traits make us unique. Certainly, your personality type shapes the early grief you are feeling.

Personality Types

Those who know you well can predict your behavior. You may be the "easy one" in the family, someone who adapts quickly and without any fuss. You may be the "grouchy one," someone who adapts slowly and with lots of complaining. You may be the "quiet one," someone who holds feelings in check. What type of personality do you have?

The classic personality types may be divided into several pairs: outgoing or reserved, aggressive or passive, dramatic or calm, optimistic or pessimistic. Most people have a mixture of these traits. Some people have one trait that dominates. This type of personality may be intense and make others uncomfortable. During early grief your personality may work for you or against you. That's why you need to **know yourself**.

Unfortunately, Clark, a health care worker in his forties, didn't know that he tended to see the dark side of things. An intelligent, educated, and productive person, Clark worked at an assisted living facility in a metropolitan area. While the manager appreciated Clark's expertise, his colleagues had a slightly different impression of Clark. "He never has anything good to say," one confided. "I'm used to his whining, but I'm tired of it."

Only his close friends knew whining was Clark's way of coping—his normal adjustment pattern. Though friends wanted to be supportive, some began to tune out his conversation. They had heard too many whiny stories. So when Clark said he thought his mother had Alzheimer's disease they didn't pay much attention to his comment. Friends couldn't tell if this was another whiny story or something to be taken seriously.

As soon as they learned Clark's mother had been diagnosed with the disease, however, his friends were there for him. They listened to his stories and tried to help Clark. Would Clark have received emotional support sooner if he had an optimistic personality? Perhaps. It's easier for family and friends to interact with an optimistic person, someone like Diane.

Her personality was the exact opposite of Clark's. In her fifties, Diane was an expert sewer, quilter, embroiderer, a talented cook, and community volunteer. She had the ability to keep an optimistic attitude in the face of adversity. Though Diane had been concerned about her husband's health for years, he refused to see a doctor.

His health was so poor that walking was difficult. Going up the stairs made him gasp for breath. Finally, he agreed to a medical check-up and test results confirmed Diane's worst fear: severe heart disease. Two sons had already died and now her husband was gravely ill. As much as she loved her husband, she knew his faults. "My husband was a stubborn man and it killed him," she said. For her husband ignored his doctor's advice. He continued to be sedentary, ate too much, and died of a heart attack several months later.

"People keep telling me I've had such a hard life," Diane said. "Well, I've had a beautiful life and my [deceased] husband

and sons are part of it." During her early grief she drew upon her personality strengths, enjoyed each day as it came, and continued her normal activities. She treasured the time she spent with her remaining child, a daughter, and stayed in close touch with friends.

Diane was glad to be alive and this positive outlook continued after her husband's death. "I'm not going to persecute myself," she declared. "I'm not just going to exist. I'm going to live my life!" Though she doesn't want to be considered as an example for others, Diane's friends see her as one. When other community residents hear Diane's story they are moved by her courage, her positive personality, and her trust in life.

You may **draw upon your personality strengths.** Try to be constructive as you tackle problems or issues. For example, even if your personality revolves around an obsessive critical approach, don't just point out problems. This can exhaust your family and friends. Instead, apply your analytic style to the crisis and try to develop carefully designed solutions or explanations.

The Age Factor

You are probably in late middle age if your parents are eighty years old or more. Anticipating the death of someone who has lived a long life is different than grieving for a younger person. "You will feel less attachment feelings than would a twenty-or-thirty year-old son or daughter who survives middle-age parents," notes Edward Myers.

There is more to the age factor. One of your parents may have already died and you may be awaiting the death of the other. Losing your remaining parent may make you feel like an orphan, which is an uncomfortable feeling at this time of life. Images of childhood may appear in your mind, so clear you think they happened yesterday.

A parent's love survives even death. **Remember your parents' love** during your early grief. Their ethics, values, interests, humor, and role models may sustain you. "I find myself repeating things my mother used to say," a daughter admitted. "Silly things like 'If you tell a lie your nose will get longer. Make sure you are wearing clean underwear. Dry the silver before it rusts.' This always made me laugh because the silver was dollar store stuff. My mother was a wonderful person and I carry her spirit in my soul."

Age is all you can think about if you are grieving for a child. You grieve for your child's lost future. You struggle with losing that child in the here and now, but also face that you will not share future experiences. Intense grief like this can tear a person, a couple, or a family apart.

Children's birthdays and parent's deaths are more than statistics, according to Rabbi Harold Kushner, author of *Who Needs God*. "They serve as ways of strengthening or diminishing the community though which we make our lives matter." What makes your life matter? It may be your relationship with the ill person, another factor that shapes your early grief.

Relationship With the Ill Person

Maybe you are grieving for someone close to you, a spouse, significant other, or sibling. In their book, *Life After Loss: The Lessons of Grief,* Vamik D. Volkan, MD and Elizabeth Zintl discuss the death of a sibling. Volkan, who is a psychiatrist, thinks his profession tends to emphasize the ambivalent feelings of sibling rivalry. But he says our siblings teach us about sharing, negotiation, companionship, and responsibility.

Your sibling's acute illness may stir up feelings of longing, guilt, and anger. The prospect of losing is sibling is more than a shock; it's a marker that shatters the childhood notion that we all grow old together. In truth, only some of us grow old together. This is a harsh reality to accept because it is a prelude of things to come.

Still, we must accept the fact that our loved ones die. **Consider your relationship with the ill person.** How long have you had this relationship? Is it a close one? Does it continue to work or is it strained? Frequently, the imperfect relationships are the hardest to leave. You not only mourn the relationship, but the possibility that it will improve. There may not be an opportunity for reconciliation.

If you are a professional or family caregiver, you have things to reconcile as well. Caregivers [health professionals] are vulnerable to the accumulated pain and suffering of early grief, according to Marion A. Humphrey, contributor to *Loss & Early grief.* Family members are also vulnerable, perhaps more so. Humphrey says family members have many adaptational tasks to work through. These tasks vary from family to family and include:

- staying involved with your loved one
- retaining separate needs from the dying person
- adapting to changing roles, such as a husband assuming a mother role and an adult child assuming a parent role
- facing your early grief
- confronting reality (You may have to go over your loved one's care plans, funeral arrangements, financial matters, and insurance documents over and over again.)
- saying goodbye to your loved one—the hardest task of all.

Complete your adaptational tasks, if possible. Make a

list and start crossing off the tasks. Do this for your loved one and for yourself because the alternative is worse. "Goodbyes left unsaid, or not completed in a way that is satisfactory to the survivor, can be devastating to the grief experience," writes Humphrey.

We need to make one last point about relationships. The death of a significant person reminds us of our own mortality. Death used to be far away and now it is closer. That is reason enough to enjoy this day. Call a friend and ask her or him to join you for lunch, go for a walk together, or just sit and talk. You may wish to talk about the roles you have in your respective families. Perhaps you have more roles than you realize.

What Is Your Role?

Your role in the dying person's life shapes early grief. Are you a parent? Grandparent? Caregiver? Mediator? Mentor? All of us have roles to play. Problems arise when new roles are added to existing ones. This may have already happened to you. A person can only juggle so many roles, as Phillip, a 60-year old professional discovered.

Phillip had a stressful job that required committee work, corporate planning sessions, continuing education, after work meetings, national and international conferences. Additionally, he was a husband, father, grandfather, and his mother's Power of Attorney. Towards the end of her life, when his mother was in the hospital and near death, he exercised this power.

"My mother signed a living will and doesn't want any special measures to be taken," he explained. "But every time there's a shift change I have to make the life or death decision again. Don't they read the chart? Why can't they leave me alone?"

While Phillip knew health professionals were trying to

save his mother's life, it was painful to be asked to make the "no special measures" decision each day. He talked with a supervising physician and urged—indeed pleaded—with him to honor his mother's wishes. It was the last time that health professionals questioned her living will. This took some of the pressure off Philip, but the pain of the experience remained with him for years.

Studies indicate that women are often the caregivers. Some societies assign this role to the youngest daughter. Women have many counteracting forces in their lives, according to Marilyn Mason, PhD, author of *Making Our Lives Our Own: A Woman's Guide to the Six Personal Challenges* of *Life.* To fit the biology of sexual maturity, childbirth, and menopause, women's lives are viewed as linear.

Mason doesn't think this model fits women's lives and prefers to see them depicted with a sphere. The seasons of life—sowing, blooming, harvesting, and regenerative—are listed on the sphere. "No growing season is ever empty," she says. Early grief can be a growing season for you. It may also be a season of additional stress.

Your role with the dying person may put you in a no-win situation. No matter what you do, no matter how hard you try, no matter how long your work, no matter how much money you spend, someone is hurt or angry. "My brother does absolutely nothing!" a tired daughter exclaimed. "I visit the nursing home every day. Who is he to criticize?"

Think about the roles that you have. You may, or may not, be surprised at the number. Perhaps you have overlooked some roles. Can you juggle all of them? Try to balance your needs with those of others. This is hard. You may have to neglect your needs for a short time to respond to an aging mother, for example, but don't ignore yourself too long.

Too Little Experience

Lack of experience also shapes early grief, as William and Sara discovered. The couple was totally unprepared for early grief when it entered their lives. William and Sara had a 17-year-old daughter and she was all any parent could hope for—pretty, bright, talented, articulate, and ambitious. The teenager planned to become a health professional or a scientist.

Her career plans, and her parent's plans for her, were dashed when she was severely injured in a skiing accident. In addition to a broken limb, the teenager sustained head trauma and lapsed into a coma. Seeing their daughter in a coma sent the couple into emotional shock. Neighbors, friends, and church members rallied to help them. Weeks passed and, with their daughter still in a coma, the couple went into deeper shock.

"Our lives were always happy," Sarah explained. "Nothing sad had ever happened to us before."

Finding the emotional resources to handle early grief was an arduous process, but the couple did it. They determined their needs, learned from others' experience, and accepted help. You may **learn from others' experience.** Their wisdom will help you to cope with the present and to plan the future.

The illness of a second child forces parents to reassess their needs. In this horrible situation they may learn from the first child's death and get more support for palliative care for the second child. While these instances are rare, it is worth noting that parents learn from life experience. Some of us, unfortunately, have too much of it. You may not realize the scope of your experience until you sit down and track it on paper.

SMILING THROUGH YOUR TEARS: ANTICIPATING GRIEF

Too Much Experience

Cumulative experience is also a factor that shapes early grief. John W. James and Frank Cherry, in a handbook about grief recovery, say grief robs us of happiness. Early grief may have done that to you. To move beyond this grief, you have to recognize and accept what you have been through. James and Cherry conduct seminars to help people recover from loss.

One of the seminar activities is to make a Loss History Graph, a horizontal line with grief events listed on it. The grief events are marked with vertical lines and the height of these lines indicates the severity of grief. You may wish to do something similar. List your early and post-death grief experiences in one column. Write the date opposite each event. Are there any close dates, or grief clusters? **Review your grief history.** As you go through it answer these questions.

- How many members of your immediate family have died?
- How many members of your extended family have died?
- Have you lost any pets?
- How many close friends have died?
- Were any of the deaths sudden and unexpected?
- Do you see any grief clusters?
- Have you learned anything from grief?

Experts say a long grief history makes you more vulnerable. Yet you may be able to make these experiences work for you. You may be someone like Jake, the patriarch of a large extended family. Jake was so beloved that distant relatives e-mailed him regularly. At 95 years of age many loved ones, including his wife, siblings, and close friends, had died. While he mourned their passing and told funny stories about these people, Jake didn't spend much time on grief. Instead, he honored their memories by living his life to the fullest.

Experience with death had taught Jake to appreciate life. Your early grief experiences may help you do the same. **Honor the dying by living your life.** In their book, *Why Me? Coping With Grief, Loss, and Change*, Rabbi Pesach Krauss and Morrie Goldfisher describe life as a "precious gift to hold with open hands." Hold this gift in your hands *and* your heart.

Conflicting Feelings

Even if you're a stable person, an emotional rock of Gibraltar, early grief causes strange feelings. Alun Jones writes about these kinds of feelings in "Actors in an Emotional Drama." Jones says people can experience several different emotions at once. You may have totally opposite feelings of hope and despair, suspense and calm, humor and sadness.

Opposite emotions like these are emotionally wrenching. You may also have new feelings of anger, self-pity, and guilt. Family members almost always have guilt feelings, according to grief expert Therese A. Rando. Even if you have been a loving, caring, and attentive person, you may still feel guilty. The result of your guilt feelings is more anxiety.

Rando says some family members feel guilty because they failed to protect a loved one from illness. Other family members feel guilty because they are going to survive their loved one. It's also common for family members to wish their loved one had died. At this point, Rando says health professionals may arrange for a guilt intervention. This process involves counseling sessions where you try to regain perspective on reality. Examining the situation with a professional will help to prevent guilt from devastating you. The time you spend with a professional now may save you time and additional guilt later. Counseling may also prepare you for grief triggers.

SMILING THROUGH YOUR TEARS: ANTICIPATING GRIEF

Grief Triggers

Just when you think your early grief is under control, something gets it going again. Another slip in your loved one's health may spark grief. Many grief triggers, things like birthday parties, holiday celebrations, and anniversaries, are obvious. But you may not be prepared for reliving your loved one's health crisis.

Co-author Harriet lives in Rochester, MN, home of Mayo Clinic. When her daughter was injured in a car crash, police called the Mayo 1 helicopter and her daughter was flown to the hospital. Harriet was familiar with the helicopter's flight paths because one was over her house. Months after the accident, whenever the helicopter flew overhead, a chill went down her spine and she had feelings of dread. The sound of the helicopter triggered Harriet's feelings of early grief.

It took her more than a year to overcome this response. How did she do it? Rather than thinking about her daughter's accident, Harriet thought about the medical crew helping others. She consciously shifted her thoughts from negative to positive. While this wasn't an easy process it became easier in time. Grief triggers can take you back in time so **watch for them.**

You can learn to overcome grief triggers. More important, you can learn to take better care of yourself. Family members may also help you. Sometimes it's easier to handle grief triggers alone than in a group. If you don't wish to attend a birthday party, family members will probably understand. Another option is going to the party for a short time and leaving early. Your family also has the option of having the party later, when you feel more secure.

Family Culture/Customs

Grief is a universal emotion, yet there are huge differences in the way people respond to it. Wolfgang Stroebe, PhD and Margaret S. Stroebe, PhD examine the relationship between culture and grief in a chapter of *Death & Identity*. Cultural differences are "attempts to provide solutions to bereavement," according to the authors, and they use Balinese culture as an example.

The Balinese may smile or laugh in response to tragic events. These people are not insensitive; they are trying to protect their health and well-being. In other cultures, the entire village may grieve for the death of an infant. This collective grief makes it easier for the sorrowful parents to show their feelings. Family customs are the stage setting for the drama of early grief.

"My father came from stoic German stock and my mother came from stiff-upper-lip British stock," a daughter said. "There wasn't much touching or hugging in our family and we were trained to hide our feelings. At an early age I learned to handle problems on my own." The behaviors you learn in childhood carry into adulthood. Volkan and Zintal make this point in their book, *Life After Loss: The Lessons of Grief.*

Each family's script draws upon its history, myths, traditions, losses, and expectations, according to the authors. "These are powerful forces and they conspire to direct a drama that compels each family member, even those who are ill-served by their roles." But you don't have to be poorly served by your family culture. You have the power to choose another path. On the other hand, if your family culture and customs work for you, **draw strength from your supportive family**. Allow the people who love you to help you. You may also draw strength from spirituality, another factor that shapes early grief.

SMILING THROUGH YOUR TEARS: ANTICIPATING GRIEF

Spirituality

Up until now you may taken spirituality for granted. Going to church, synagogue, or mosque was just something you did, part of your routine. But the pain of early grief may force you to tap your spiritual reserves. In his book *Who Needs God*, Rabbi Harold Kushner says spiritual beliefs come from a desire to understand the world. Not only is the world imperfect, Kushner explains, it often makes no sense at all.

Spiritual people see the world through the prism of beliefs. This is more than a matter of seeing the glass of life as half empty or half full," according to Kushner. "It is whether faith and experience have taught us to look at a glass that is nearly empty, like Hagar's water bottle, and believe that there are resources in the world capable of refilling it."

Despite your strong faith, you may doubt your spirituality and struggle to understand why a loved one is dying. You might want to explore your thoughts with a chaplain or spiritual advisor. They are familiar with even the most devoted people having their faith shaken by emotionally distressing events. Try to turn to your spiritual beliefs for comfort even if you have ambivalent feelings.

Journalist Betty Rollin is a breast cancer survivor. She talked frankly about her illness on the "Quiet Triumphs" television program. Being diagnosed with breast cancer made her realize that she had to get out of an unhappy marriage. If she was going to die, Rollin figured she would make the most of her remaining days. Rollin obtained a divorce, had two mastectomies, and breast reconstruction. These experiences changed her view of life. Each year is a small victory and Rollin is humbly grateful to be alive. "I got a lot more grateful because I noticed I was breathing," she said.

Look upon early grief as an opportunity to strengthen your spirituality. Dr. Robert Veniga, in his book *A Gift of Hope*, says faith helps us to let go of fear and takes us to new dimensions of hope, possibility, and peace. Daily meditation may help you to find that peace. Life does get easier, Veniga says, and sometimes "the sacred speaks through other people." Listen for these words and take these healing steps.

Healing Steps

- Know yourself.
- Draw upon your personality strengths.
- Remember your parents' love.
- Consider your relationship with the ill person.
- Think about the roles you have.
- Learn from others' experience.
- Review your grief history.
- Complete adaptational tasks, if possible.
- Honor the dying by living your life.
- Watch for grief triggers.
- Draw strength from a supportive family.
- Find comfort in spirituality.

CHAPTER 5
Early Grief's Symptoms and Stages

Grief drives men into habits of serious reflection, sharpens the understanding and softens the heart.

John Adams writing to Thomas Jefferson

SMILING THROUGH YOUR TEARS: ANTICIPATING GRIEF

The symptoms of early grief develop over time. Despite variations in intensity, people who are going through early grief share common symptoms. You may think the symptoms have disappeared and are gone forever, only to have them turn up again. Being able to **recognize the symptoms** will make your early grief journey easier.

Common Symptoms

Shock is usually the first symptom of early grief and it affects everything you do. From the outside your behavior may look normal. On the inside you may have a constant feeling of shock. What's happening to you? Early grief has many symptoms and they are listed below. You may wish to put a checkmark by the ones you have experienced.

- Denial
- Emotional numbness
- Nervous, restless behavior
- Ongoing anxiety and dread
- Mood swings
- Crying spells and a choked feeling in your throat
- Persistent feeling of sadness
- Depression
- Anger
- Ambivalent feelings
- Inability to concentrate and poor retention
- Constant forgetfulness
- Disorganized and confused behavior
- Increasing vulnerability
- Changes in your health (See chapter six for more information.)

- Rushing, busy behaviors and hyperactivity
- Poor eating habits
- Interrupted sleep and/or sleep deprivation
- Fatigue and/or exhaustion
- Feeling disconnected and alone

The early grief of terrorism includes these symptoms and more. According to the American Red Cross the additional symptoms are suspicion, flashbacks, fear, an obsessive need for information, and memory problems. Add all the symptoms together and you have a life struggle.

Has anyone commented on your early grief symptoms? Do they understand them? Do you understand them? The symptoms of early grief may fluctuate. Be cautious about making major life decisions such as quitting a career to care for a loved one. Look for a compromise if you feel you must make a decision.

John S. Rolland, author of *Living Beyond Loss: A Death in the Family,* says the emotions associated with early grief are intense. Perhaps you have noticed this in yourself. "Emotional expression often fluctuates between these more difficult feelings and others, such as a heightened sense of being alive," he writes.

When it comes to handling grief Stephenson thinks society works against us. He notes that we live in a high-tech world and many of us enjoy finding solutions to difficult problems. Solutions prove our technical mastery; indeed, we may feel like we can master anything. Much to our surprise, we discover that we can't master early grief or its stages. It's frustrating, to say the least.

Stages of Grief

You will understand early grief better if you **know**

its stages. Some researchers use the post-death categories defined by Elizabeth Kubler-Ross: isolation/anger, bargaining, depression, and acceptance. As more is learned about early grief, however, these phases seem to be shifting.

Since early grief is an inexact process the stages are not precise. The stages may overlap, be delayed, or accelerate. Some experts divide early grief into three stages: sadness and anger, disorganization and reorganization, readjustment and recovery. *Death & Identity* chapter author John S. Stephenson, PhD thinks we spend most of our time in the disorganized phase.

Before early grief you may have thought you had lots of time to set goals, work towards them, and reach them. Life stretched out endlessly before you. Now, with the onset of early grief, you find that your time is limited. Stephenson thinks this understanding of time may be the basis of all early grief. Is it the basis of yours? Time is paramount for parents who are grieving for a seriously ill child. Children's Hospital Boston has a Web site for families. The Pediatric Advanced Care team posts the phases of early grief on the Web site to help families. Here are the phases (or stages) with some added comments.

Stage one: Realization that death is inevitable. You may become sad, depressed, and angry during this phase. Grief experts say your anger may be directed towards the person who is dying because he or she is deserting you. Anger may also be directed at health professionals, at disease, and maybe yourself for not coping better.

Stage two: Concern for the dying person. Time becomes a problem for you and the dying person. While you want to spend as much time as you can with your loved one, you must tend to your own life. Family members may disagree, get into arguments, and even squabble over the ill person's possessions during this phase.

Stage three: Rehearsal for death. You say goodbye to your loved one and may start to make funeral arrangements or confirm pre-made arrangements. If you have arguments to settle and apologies to make you will probably do it at this time.

Stage four: Family members and friends start to imagine life without a loved one. For many, this is the most painful phase of early grief. You worry about the future. Will you survive without this person? What kind of life will you have? This is a time of true acceptance.

The Web site says we are all different and go through early grief in our own ways. Early grief affects every family member and you may help each other. **Set up a mutual support system.**

This coping tool can shore you up, keep you going, and keep the family system intact. An intact support system helps you during the living-dying interval. What is this interval and why is it important?

The Living-Dying Interval

Early grief continues through the living-dying interval, the time between the knowledge of death and actual death. This interval prolongs the symptoms and stages of early grief. Your grief may flare and burst into flames like the embers of a forgotten campfire. Fortunately, your mind has not forgotten all of the emotional work you have done.

Patricia S. Jones, PhD and Ida M. Martinson, PhD, write about caregivers' grief in their article, "The Experience of Bereavement in Caregivers of Family Members with Alzheimer's Disease." They interviewed relatives whose loved ones had died of the disease. Thirteen people joined in the study, nine females and four males, ranging in age from 38 to 76.

Data from the taped interviews were analyzed. Seven caregivers (54 percent) said their grief was greatest during the caregiving time. The researchers described this time as a 10-year funeral. One caregiver said she grieved constantly "because when you think there is nothing left to lose, you lose a little more." Part of the caregivers' grief was related to saying goodbye or not being able to say goodbye because of a loved one's profound dementia.

Edward Myers, in his book *When Parents Die: A Guide for Adults*, has a personal view of the living-dying interval. When his mother was extremely ill, Myers said "each new crisis—further bleeding, a brain abscess, meningitis, kidney damage, cardiac arrhythmias, epilepsy, pneumonia—left her worse off than before."

During the last year of her life his mother was totally helpless—paralyzed, unable to communicate, in and out of coma. The living-dying interval was searing emotional pain for Myers, the kind of pain that stays with you for the rest of your days. "The way she died affected me more than the death itself," he writes. The living-dying interval causes problems for patients and family members. Each problem can be a crisis itself.

Your loved one may be dying right before your eyes and it's terrible to witness. That's bad enough, but your loved one may also go through a series of remissions and relapses. During this time you may be involved in making such treatment decisions as whether to start dialysis. You consider the doctors' recommendations, but the final decision rests with you. How much time will treatment "buy?" What are the side effects of treatment? Have you considered all of your loved one's wishes and directives? Do family members agree with your treatment decisions?

People with chronic illness may linger for weeks. You live in fear day after day after day. Insurance may not cover all of the medical costs and you may be haunted by financial worries. You loved one may have outstanding hospital bills, medication bills, private nursing bills, ambulance bills, transportation bills, and burial costs yet to be paid.

Make allowances for the living-dying interval. Most families pull together during this time, while others break apart. Even for close families the living-dying interval can be shaky ground. Family systems differ and, though you love your family, you can't control all family members or your family system, so watch for cracks.

Small cracks in the family relationships may turn into serious breaks. The unpredictable time line only makes things worse. Avoid these cracks, if you can, because you have a lot of grief work ahead of you. Focus on the strengths of your family and pull together, if possible, because nothing can replace a solid family system.

Your Family

While you're going through the stages of early grief you still have to go about your daily tasks—grocery shopping, cleaning, laundry, finding sitters for kids, and paying bills. You may not do some of these tasks because you want to be with your loved one constantly. But Kubler-Ross says family members need to let off some emotional steam to prevent resentments from developing.

"Just as we have to breathe in and breathe out, people have to 'recharge their batteries' outside the sickroom at times, live a normal life from time to time; we cannot function efficiently in the constant awareness of the illness," she writes. While the dying patient's problems come to an end, Kubler-Ross says the family's problems may be just beginning. Family members, including you, may try to protect the dying person by covering up feelings. According to Kubler-Ross, communication is important for the living *and* the dying. Sharing your feelings may be a relief for all concerned and help your loved one to "die with equanimity."

Even if your family has good communication the rules of communication may change. Family members may change the rules to protect their loved ones and themselves. Froma Walsh, PhD and Monica McGoldrick MSW detail these changes in their book *Living Beyond Loss: Death in the Family.* As they explain, "When a parent has had a heart attack, the family rule of open communication may shift to one of conflict avoidance to protect against a fatal occurrence."

Poll your family members to see if communication is working. If it isn't working, get suggestions from them and **take steps to improve communication.** These steps may include such things as caller ID, a speakerphone for the hearing impaired, a fax machine, and getting an e-mail address. Family members may agree to share the costs of these items. You may also put things in writing for family members.

Recurring Early Grief

Though experts know the symptoms and phases of early grief, they can't accurately predict when it will recur. Alicia found this out during her husband's successive illnesses. His series of illnesses began when he fell on an icy sidewalk and developed a headache. The headache didn't seem severe and, because he had no other symptoms, the couple went on a skiing trip as planned. After they returned her husband said his headache had gotten worse. A CAT scan revealed a very large hematoma in his brain, which was drained surgically.

"Everything seemed to heal all right," his wife recalled. "Things seemed to be back to normal." No other symptoms appeared during the next few years and the couple continued their skiing trips. On the way home from one trip they stopped at a motel. During their stay she discovered that her husband couldn't get out of the bathtub.

Alicia helped him step out of the tub, called his doctor at home, and made an appointment for a physical exam the next day. He was diagnosed with a neurological disease and spent four months in the hospital. While Alicia was concerned about him, she wasn't overly concerned because he was getting excellent care. Doctors thought her husband would recover within a year.

But Alicia became very worried about her husband's behavior in the hospital. He watched little television before and now he watched it constantly. He was so uninterested in outside events that he wouldn't even open the mail. Finally, Alicia asked doctors to give her husband a series of mental tests. The results: low to normal on intellectual functions and a diagnosis of Parkinson's disease.

"You settle into a pattern and suddenly you're jarred loose again," she said. Each of her husband's successive illnesses forced Alicia to find new ways of coping. Her early grief grew progressively worse. "Once I knew Parkinson's was the case and the disease wasn't going to go away, I really began to grieve," she said. "I thought to myself, 'This is the way it's going to end.'"

Ironically, Alicia's husband died of a stroke. Her story is more than a story of multiple illnesses, it is a story of recurring early grief. **Prepare yourself for recurring grief** as best as you can. While you're at it you may as well prepare yourself for delayed grief because it comes with the territory. Delayed grief is an odd response and it may have happened to you already.

Delayed Grief

Perhaps you have been grieving for two, five, or even 10 years. Because you have so many responsibilities you push early grief to the back of your mind. This is called delayed grief. Usually the term is associated with post-death feelings, but people with early grief also delay their feelings. Each situation is different.

Lillian, the woman you read about earlier and whose mother died before her husband, put her early grief aside for a year. "I tried not to cry in front of him because I was in the role of trying to be strong," she explained. "I cried in front of my friends but I couldn't do that to him." So she kept pushing her early grief feelings back into her mind to avoid handling these feelings.

Still, the couple managed to discuss her future as a single parent. "We put our faith in a higher power," she said, "trusting that things would work out, trusting that life would be OK. There was a plan for my life, a plan for my son's life, and a plan for my husband's life." Though Lillian experienced some early grief, it returned in full force after her husband died.

"I think I'm going through early grief all over again," she said. "I'm just starting to move beyond it. I call this time my post-traumatic stress syndrome. It's really weird. When I'm done I think I will really grieve for my husband." Lillian's emotional honesty, stability, and grieving style served her well through her husband's illness and death.

Rebecca J. Walker and her colleagues examine delayed grief in their article, "Anticipatory Grief and Aids: Strategies for Intervening with Caregivers." There seems to be an optimal period of early grief, the authors say, anywhere between six and eighteen months. Due to the nature of AIDS and HIV infection, the course of treatment may extend beyond this time frame.

"The duration of the illness and the stigmatization and multiple losses associated with the disease may impede the caregiver's ability to effectively engage in the grief process," they write. Well-meaning people may try to rush you through early grief. They may even tell you to start a new intimate relationship because that's what your loved one "would want."

What ever your loved one's illness is, you take some emotional risks when you delay early grief. It can be difficult to think about a death that hasn't happened yet. Take the time to recover emotionally. **Try not to delay your grief.** Your bottled up pain has to come out and sooner is better than later. When you delay grief you risk an emotional explosion and you don't want that.

Styles of Grieving

How do you grieve? Alla Bozarth-Campbell writes about grieving styles in *Life is Goodbye, Life is Hello: Grieving Well Through All Kinds of Loss.* He describes several post-death styles: hero, martyr, crazyperson (a compound word), and fool. You may rely more on one role or use all of them to cope with early grief.

Bozarth-Campbell thinks the hero denies fear and is really a mock hero. The hero thinks he or she can handle things alone. Being the family hero makes other family members angry because it ignores their feelings and actions. You may not be the only one in the family who is trying to help. The hero role also has its pitfalls.

SMILING THROUGH YOUR TEARS: ANTICIPATING GRIEF

You may become a focus of family resentment. Family members may think you're responsible for everything that doesn't go smoothly and not credit you for the things that do. Anyone who has experienced this kind of resentment will tell you that it's a lose-lose situation. These resentments may continue long after your loved one's demise.

Some grieving people are martyrs to the cause. This style of grieving has problems too, according to Bozarth-Campbell. He thinks martyrs turn their guilt and energy inward and may act impulsively. "Causing pain to oneself is a substitute for surviving the reality of loss," he explains. Over-commitment is another problem associated with being a martyr. Without consulting others, a martyr may meet with lawyers, plan the funeral, write the obituary, and select the gravestone. These actions may not match the dying person's wishes. Again, this kind of behavior ignores other people's feelings and actions.

Bozarth-Campbell says the crazyperson is explosive, attacking, and blames everyone else. Their volatile feelings ignite quickly. Maybe you're seen the crazyperson in action. This person cuts in line, wants instant attention, demeans the staff, and tries to upset you and other bystanders. You wish you were somewhere else.

The researcher doesn't mention the super-responsible person, yet another grieving style. Life events, such as being without family support and getting financial aid for the dying person, force this role on unsuspecting people. You may pay a high price for being super-responsible and it can lead to the hero role that was detailed earlier.

And the researcher doesn't mention the activist role. Activists work through their grief by helping others. You may help to raise funds for heart research, become a hospital volunteer, or start a discussion group. This displacement of feelings gets you out of yourself and connects you with others. After your loved one has died you may continue this role.

When all is said and done, it's best to **find your own style** of grieving. Watch for the symptoms, note the stages, and keep on trudging. Be sure to check with other people from time to time because early grief can make you feel disconnected. This kind of aloneness may lead you down a destructive path. You don't want to become isolated and alone.

Isolation and Aloneness

Though aloneness isn't a stage of early grief, it is woven into the grief process. Dr. Robert Buckman, author of *"I Don't Know What to Say: How to Help and Support Someone Who is Dying,"* thinks isolation [or aloneness] is part of modern society. He cites some of the causes of our isolation in his book.

The elderly rarely die at home these days, Buckman says, they die in a hospital or hospice. Our society has high expectations for health and longevity. Buckman calls this the "They will find a cure" outlook. Some of us value material things so much that we lose touch with reality. Last, some of us are going through a spiritual crisis.

Aloneness can lead to depression, so you need to take steps to counter this feeling. Those who have completed early grief say affinity groups, such as hobby clubs, church guilds and Alcoholics Anonymous, helped them greatly. They also say honesty is the best approach to grief work.

Be yourself. You don't need to smile every moment of the day to hide your grief. Tell people what you're going through. Try to explain your early grief in a few short sentences. "I let it all hang out," a wife said. "I didn't care what people thought. They couldn't grieve for me. It was my grief and I had to grieve in my own way. I'm still grieving and I'm getting better."

Healing Steps

- Recognize the symptoms of early grief.
- Know the stages.
- Set up a mutual support system.
- Make allowances for the living-dying interval.
- Take steps to improve family communication.
- Share your feelings.
- Prepare for recurring early grief.
- Try not to delay your grief.
- Find your own grieving style.
- Guard against aloneness.
- Be yourself.

CHAPTER 6
Responses to Early Grief

*Although the world is full of suffering,
it is also full of the overcoming of it.*

Helen Keller

SMILING THROUGH YOUR TEARS: ANTICIPATING GRIEF

How do people respond to early grief? People are different and family members may not respond as you do. Friends may respond in similar or very different ways. To set the stage, let's look at behavior and health, two major response areas. You may be experiencing behavior and health changes right now.

Changes in Behavior

Once early grief enters your life it becomes part of your life—you can't avoid it. Every day, every week, every month begins and ends with early grief, and it wears you down. Maggie Callanan and Patricia Kelley, authors of *Final Gifts: Understanding the Special Awareness, Needs and Communication of the Dying*, talk about the exhaustion of early grief.

"Coping with terminal illness is more than hard work—it's all-consuming and creeps into every corner of your life," they say. "It's an exhausting, emotional roller coaster ride."

The solution is to get off the roller coaster, but you can't get off, and early grief takes its toll. Without any warning (and often at the worst times) you may burst into tears. You may have mood swings, a short attention span, a feeling of restlessness, and lose track of details. Trying harder to remember details simply doesn't work. "I used to be pretty sharp," one caregiver said. "Now my mind wanders all over the place. It's very upsetting."

Some people become hyper to cope with early grief and take on too much. They race from one activity to another, complete them as fast as they can, and race on to the next. For even a moment, these people are afraid to slow down for fear their thoughts will catch up with them. Hyper activity is their "protective shield."

Sooner or later, though, you must confront your painful thoughts. Will my loved one die today? How will I react when that happens? If I feel this badly now, how will I feel after he or she is gone forever? You know time will answer these questions, but the waiting is hard, painful and tough.

If you've been grieving a long time you may not feel much emotion. You're numb. Psychiatrists call this a "flat affect." The stress of early grief has wrung your feelings out of you. Your feelings hardly change from one day to the next and you don't care. This is scary because you really love and care so much.

You may not feel like yourself at all. The extreme changes in your behavior may push family and friends away. People you counted on may refuse to help you at a time when you need them most. Their lack of help hurts you, but you may **find a safe retreat or refuge from distress and pain.**

Think of some retreats now. A special place, such as a cabin in the woods, may comfort you. New activities, such as joining the church choir or reading to kids, may be comforting as well. As you search for safe retreats keep telling yourself, "I will get through this pain." Though you may not believe it now, you *will* get through it.

Each of us walks along the early grief path at our own pace. It's such a tiring journey that you may start to withdraw socially, but pulling back isn't good for you. Withdrawing from social contacts sets you up for a lonely, bleak, isolated life and you certainly don't need that. You need just the opposite.

Keeping social contacts gives you a way to heal. So get some rest, regroup, and choose your contacts. A few hours with friends can renew your energy for the weeks to come and you will need this energy. While it's normal to be preoccupied with the dying person's health, you need to take care of your own health, too. Have you noticed any changes in your health? Have family and friends mentioned any changes to you? Are you doing things to stay healthy? Early grief may have already changed your health a great deal.

Changes in Health

Perhaps you have bags under your eyes, a sign of exhaustion, and other health changes. Sherry E. Showalter, MSW, in her article "Walking With Grief: The Trail of Tears in a World of AIDS" details the physical responses to grief. "Survivors of multiple losses and cumulative grief are susceptible to chronic illness, exhaustion, and increased stress," she says.

You're not going to be able to care for anyone else unless you care for yourself. Certainly, you don't want to become a burden to a family that's already burdened. If you're taking care of yourself that's great. But if you've been neglecting yourself it's time **get a physical exam.** You may be run down, anemic, or have these physical responses to early grief.

- Poor eating habits (skipping meals, eating junk food)
- Weight gain (from nervous eating and eating on the run)
- Weight loss (forgetting to eat or eating unbalanced meals)
- Poor sleep (disturbed and/or interrupted)
- Pale skin (not getting outside, fatigue)
- Red eyes (from crying or lack of sleep)
- General fatigue (no energy for anything)

Seeing things in writing helps you get a clearer picture of how you're doing health-wise. Jot down your physical and behavioral responses to early grief now. Date the list, tuck it in the back of the book, and look at it in a few months. Now let's look at some other early grief responses, starting with panic.

The Panic Response

It's scary enough to feel panic, but it's really scary if you have never felt panic before. Panic is a normal response to grief, explains Granger E. Westberg in his book, *Good Grief*. "Because we know so little about the nature of grief, we become panicky when it strikes us," he says, "and this serves to throw us into deeper despondency."

Harriet panicked after her daughter was severely injured in a car crash. She remembers bargaining with God while her daughter lay in a coma for two and a half days. In exchange for her daughter's recovery Harriet offered to be the critically injured person and she prayed for her daughter's recovery. The sequence of her thoughts was something like this.

Please let her live.

Please let her wake up.

Please let her be as smart as she was before.

Please let her walk.

Please let her have a normal life.

Please let her be happy.

Usually a calm, stable, and adaptable person, Harriet was terrified by the panic she felt. The panic was doubly terrifying because she had been in crisis before and had good coping skills. Were her emotional reserves gone? Life has many lessons to teach us and she found new emotional reserves to draw upon. Harriet was surprised by these reserves because she didn't know she had them.

You may be grieving for more than one person or event, so it's important to **find ways to relax and detach**. Detachment means you're able to get away mentally. It can help you cope

SMILING THROUGH YOUR TEARS: ANTICIPATING GRIEF

with early grief, provided it occurs at an appropriate time and is short-lived. How does detachment work?

A middle-aged daughter may hastily catch an airline flight because of urgent news that her father is having a heart attack. At that moment, nothing in her control will make the plane fly faster or increase the chances that the cardiac unit will save her father's life. She needs to take care of herself and preserve her emotional resources.

During the flight the daughter gazes out the window and sees soft, fluffy clouds that go on for miles. They look like the bubbles in a warm soothing bath. For a time, she imagines herself floating in this beautiful setting, floating far above the ground, without any worries. Before too long, these thoughts are swept away by thoughts of her father's medical problem. Yet for a brief time, she was able to escape this crisis. Without interfering with her response to her mother's needs or the needs of family members, the daughter's brief detachment helped her preserve her energies.

But detachment becomes a problem when it lasts too long and overlaps with denial. People may dissociate—they feel like they are viewing their own actions and behavior from another place. Some describe having an out of body experience, when they watch themselves interact with others, yet feel removed from the situation.

Detachment can last so long that it interferes with relationships. Family members may notice a vacant expression or wonder if the person is really listening. Over time, this may cause them to worry or feel angry about being ignored. In severe cases, the dissociated person may feel out of control and scared that they're not in control of their behavior. Though this person acts out with anger or wrenching sobs, he or she doesn't feel connected or responsible for this behavior.

This may go on for some time. Jo-Eileen Gyulay, RN, PhD, author of "Grief Responses," says time is a griever's gift and enemy. "In anticipatory grief, time is the gift of every moment," she says, "yet the enemy that is stealing his child." You may feel like time is stealing your parent, spouse, or friend.

No matter whom you are grieving for, you must accept the fact that time will take your loved one from you. This can be such a shock that you go into denial. Your mind slips out of contact with the reality. Denial is a common response to early grief, especially when you first hear the shocking news. The first thoughts that come to mind may be, "I don't believe it. This can't be happening."

Denial

Denial is the unconscious process of allowing your thoughts to drift to other topics. Edward, the father of a 10 year-old boy, went into denial after his son was injured in a bike accident. Instead of thinking about his son's extensive injuries, Edward thought about taking his son swimming next summer. He went into denial.

People who are in denial may come up with a variety of excuses to avoid the truth. Lori Wiener, PhD and her colleagues list some of these excuses in their article, "The HIV Infected Child: Parental Responses and Psychosocial Implications." They use these sentences to illustrate denial.

- "Things aren't as bad as I thought."
- "Maybe the doctor got the chart confused with somebody else's."
- "They'll come up with a cure."

You may have had similar thoughts and others as well. "I think the lab technicians mixed up the samples." "We picked the wrong doctor." "This hospital isn't equipped to handle a case like this." Denial saps your energy, the same energy that you need in order to cope. Instead of denying early grief, a healthier response would be to **get accurate information.** There are many ways to do this.

Start by asking the doctor or doctors to explain the situation again. Ask the hospital or clinic for information about the disease. Make use of the hospital's patient education library. Benefit from hospital/hospice services: patient escort, patient advocate, interpreters, shuttle bus service, and others. Contact national health organizations, such as the American Heart Association and American Cancer Society, and request information. Talk with a family member, friend, or member of your religious community who has completed the early grief process. You may also find information on health Web sites.

Though you may not be able to process all of this information at once, you will remember some of it, and you can read the rest later. Once you have gathered information, store it in a file cabinet, portable file, or desk drawer, and label the space. You may write "Hospice Info," for example. This will help you to find the information later.

Anger

Early grief can make anyone angry. You may be angry unhelpful relatives, at friends who don't understand early grief, and at God for allowing this pain to come to you. Anger will continue to build unless you find ways to ventilate, and this may take some time. Let's face it—anger can be a difficult emotion to process. Getting angry at a sick person makes you feel awful. What can you do with your anger? Where does anger go?

Clinical psychologist Harriet Braiker, PhD, answers this question in her book, *Getting Up When You're Feeling Down.*

Braiker says anger goes in three directions: towards the person or object, back to ourselves, or towards an unrelated person or object, a response called displacement. People who displace their feelings misdirect them to other targets.

A man who is upset that his wife needs frequent trips to the clinic for cancer chemotherapy may displace his anger at the parking attendant who is slow in counting change. "You're not playing with a full deck!" he yells at the attendant, a sentence that implies stupidity. Responses like these are disturbing to witness.

Over time the man may feel remorse for his nasty behavior. **Accept your anger and keep it from hurting others.** Try to talk about your anger. "I spend so much time on my mother that there's no time left for me," one caregiver admitted. "I don't have a personal life any more." Don't let your anger fester and build because it will catch up with you.

Hiding Your Emotions

Since you don't know when your emotions will catch you, you may be caught off-guard like Barbara. Barbara took care of her 80-year old mother lovingly and constantly. "My mother had to go to the emergency room again," she said. "I've already been through this many times with her and this time wasn't good. On the way to the hospital I cried in the car and kept on crying in the emergency room. I couldn't stop."

An emotional dam had burst inside Barbara's mind and she knew it. "I've been over-riding my emotions," she admitted. "You can only do that so long."

Perhaps you have been over-riding your emotions. This can be dangerous and, if it goes on too long, your feelings may blow up or collapse. People can suddenly feel rage and direct it towards loved ones who are also suffering. They may spend hours in bed, hesitant to get up each day. They may turn to food for comfort. They may numb their feelings with alcohol or drugs. All of these behaviors cause more harm than good.

You need to **find an outlet for emotions so they don't remain suppressed.** Think about your outlets now. Are they working well? Pretty well? Poorly? Do you need new ones? Family members and friends who have completed the entire grief process, from early to post-death grief, may suggest some outlets for your emotions.

Am I Going Crazy?

Early grief can make you do crazy things. You may forget to buy bread and milk, the reason you went to the grocery store. You may be in the checkout line and discover that you forgot your wallet. You may confuse the days of the week and forget appointments. Small mistakes like these add up and make you worry about your mental health.

A dreaded question keeps coming to mind: Am I going crazy? You wouldn't be the first person to ask yourself this question. Many who have experienced early grief have wondered if they were going crazy. You may ask yourself other questions, too. Why can't I stop crying? Why can't I turn my mind off? Why can't I have some peace? Will I ever be able to control my emotions again? All are hard questions and finding the answers will be hard.

You may not find the answers to them on your own. It's of critical importance to **get answers to your questions from someone you trust.** Your goal is to keep moving forward on your healing path. Asking for help takes honesty and courage, so don't be ashamed of it. The answers to your questions can get you moving beyond a life on hold.

Life on Hold

People put their lives on hold when they're out of options. Edward Myers writes about life on hold in his book, *When Parents Die: A Guide for Adults.* Even under the best of circumstances a life on hold disrupts most families according to Myers. "If your sick parent has been hospitalized or placed in a nursing home, then [your] visits, consultations with doctors, and related errands have undoubtedly interrupted your normal activities."

Perhaps your life is on hold. In the mirror you see the same person, yet you feel like you are living someone else's life. Most of the familiar things in your life, your weekly golf game, for example, have been eliminated. The days are racing by, gone forever, and there's nothing you can do about it. You can only stand this so long.

An elderly grandmother, who lived in a retirement community, developed a chronic illness. Because the illness wasn't severe she continued to live in her apartment. As time passed, however, the woman became increasingly manipulative. Every time her adult daughter planned to go on a trip with her husband the grandmother would have a "spell" and wind up in the nursing care unit. This happened so many times the couple gave up.

"We're stuck," the daughter said. "We won't leave town again until my mother dies." Only friends who had been through a similar experience understood the daughter's reaction. She loved her mother so much that she would do anything for her, even put her life on hold. If your life is on hold, try to retain some normal and pleasant activities without feeling guilty. This won't happen overnight.

Resolving guilt takes time, effort, and reflection. To dispel guilt, you may need to find a way to think about other things. Remember to take care of your own needs, such as a quiet hour of reading at the library, away from the noise and confusion of life. You may have to find outside help. Arrange for a visiting nurse or enroll your failing parent in adult day care.

Your county Social Services department can tell you about available services, which ones fit your needs best, and if you qualify for financial aid. Ask a family member to give you a break from hospital or hospice visits. An increasing number of churches have parish nurses and the nurse may be able to find people to help you. Act on your own behalf because you can't live a life on hold for very long.

Sublimation

Another response to early grief is sublimation, the redirection of socially unacceptable impulses into acceptable channels. A family whose son is dying of AIDS, for example, may become devoted to fundraising for AIDS research. Though the research probably won't happen quickly enough to help their son, they pour their energy into helping others who face the same crisis.

Displacement may be reworked into sublimation, a more beneficial response for you and society.

Sublimation or not, the day-to-day stress of early grief may cause you to lose track of details. You make lists and leave them behind or lose them. One after the other, you keep missing the details, and wonder if you've missed something important. You miss so many details that you wonder if your mind has become a sieve.

Missing the Details

There's so much to think about, so much to do, that details slip from your mind. A week after her mother died, Harriet missed an important detail. She was giving a birthday dinner for her older daughter and, to make dinner festive, bought a helium balloon with a birthday cake on the front. She tied the balloon to a dining room chair.

Later that day, when she was fixing salad in the kitchen, her five-year-old grandson approached her. "Grandma, there's a one and a six on the balloon," he said. "You know, a sixteen."

"That's nice," she answered, continuing with dinner preparations. Seconds later her grandson's words registered in Harriet's mind and she rushed into the dining room. On the reverse side of the balloon there was a 16 and the words "Happy Sweet Sixteen." Harriet could hardly believe her eyes—or her mistake—yet she could laugh at herself. "I can't believe I bought a Sweet Sixteen balloon for my 35 year old daughter!" she exclaimed.

"Hey, it's the thought that counts," her daughter replied, "and it's still a birthday balloon." This story illustrates the danger of over-extending yourself. Try to **pace yourself and avoid doing too much.** Sometimes, though, you have to proceed with your plans. In these instances you may ask for help, postpone things, or eliminate them all together. Take care of yourself as you go through early grief.

Ignoring Your Needs

Many people ignore their own needs and you may be one of them. It happens before you know it. So much time and energy are spent on the dying person there's nothing left for you and your needs fade into the background. This isn't to say you mind doing this. In fact, you may derive satisfaction of doing your "job."

But problems can arise—serious, life-threatening problems—when needs are ignored too long.

A husband was so focused on caring for his wife with

breast cancer that he didn't go to the doctor for preventive medical care. It proved to be a fatal mistake. He had a ruptured abdominal aortic aneurysm and ended up dying before his wife. Surgery could have potentially prevented his death, but he neglected his own needs and his health.

Be aware of your needs and try to meet them. You have different needs at different times in your life. With practice, you will be able to spot your needs—a change of scene, creative projects, exercise, what ever they may be. Seek guidance from others to remind yourself not to overlook your own needs.

Family members and friends can help you. A friend may know someone who could do home repairs for you, for example. This might be a good time to assess your personal needs. What are they? How many have you met? How many have you ignored? Are your needs changing? Do friends see needs that you don't?

Loss of Reality

Some people who are going through early grief lose touch with reality. Though it happens rarely, when it does, events may be traumatic or even bizarre. Consider this real-life story.

For months a husband grieved for his beloved wife, who had a terminal illness, and his early grief became unbearable. Unable to envision a life without his wife and female companionship, he developed a crush on a widowed neighbor. While he didn't know her well, the man kept thinking about her, to the point of obsession.

Two days after his wife's funeral he went to the woman's house, rang the doorbell and, when she answered, handed her a bouquet of flowers. "I am interested in you and I hope to marry you," he blurted.

The woman was stunned. "Excuse me?" she asked.

"I've been thinking about this a long time," he explained, "and I would like to marry you."

"This isn't appropriate," she replied. "I hardly know you and I can't marry you."

Now it was the man's turn to be stunned. He couldn't understand her refusal because he had lost touch with reality. **Ask family members and friends to serve as reality checks** if you suspect you're losing touch with reality. Your doctor may also serve as a reality check. A reality check can get you headed in a healthier direction and help you avoid depression.

Depression

Early grief can make you lose control of your life and push you into depression. You may not realize you're depressed. Contrary to myth, depressed people smile, tell jokes, and laugh at other people's jokes. Their smiles help to hide the symptoms of depression from others. In fact, these behaviors may hide depression from you.

You may develop mysterious medical problems without clear signs of underlying disease, like headaches, back pain, limb pain, nausea, and dizziness. These symptoms are suspicious, especially if they're new and were not seen before your early grief began. Elderly people may express their depression with agitation.

Bud was a slightly confused, 75-year old man who lived in a nursing home. When his roommate became ill and was taken by ambulance to the hospital, Bud became upset. He didn't know if his roommate would return or why he had these feelings of dread. Despite his inability to describe his feelings, he could feel the dread, and would rock in a chair to get rid of his restless feelings. He rocked back and forth for hours, moaning softly. Bud's behavior bothered the other nursing home residents but, when he was asked to stop, could do it only for a short time. If this kind of behavior lasts for two weeks, it could be depression that warrants professional help.

Children may express their depression with hyperactivity. A little girl who has learned that her grandfather has a brain tumor may run around non-stop at recess. Restless in class and at home, she can't stay calm and quiet when she visits her grandfather in the hospital. When this behavior doesn't improve, the teacher asks her parents to get professional counseling for their daughter. Depression may be the underlying cause of this behavior.

Like the little girl and the elderly man, depression may be the underlying cause of your behavior. **Learn to spot the symptoms of depression.** This checklist with added comments is from the National Alliance for the Mentally Ill (NAMI) Web site. The checklist is aimed at kids, but it could also help you, because the basic symptoms are the same.

Feelings

Sadness (which may go on for a long time)
Emptiness (You may feel stuck in place.)
Hopelessness (The future may look dark or non-existent.)
Guilt (for being tired, for being angry at the ill person)
Not enjoying everyday pleasures (You just don't have the energy.)

Thinking

Difficulty in concentrating (discussed in an earlier chapter)

Difficulty in making decisions (It may take you a while to realize this.)

Difficulty in completing tasks (This may also take a while to recognize.)

Physical Problems

Headaches (stress headaches and migraine)
Stomachaches (and heartburn)
Joint or backaches (Other parts of your body may ache as well.)
Lack of energy (You may be physically exhausted.)
Sleep problems (interrupted sleep or lack of sleep)
Weight gain or loss

Behavioral Problems

Feeling irritable (Family members may steer clear of you.)
Wanting to be alone (However, you may need time to think.)
Difficulty in getting along with others
Dropping hobbies and activities (I can't do this now approach.)
Alcohol and/or drug abuse

Make an appointment with your doctor if you think you are depressed. There are therapies and medications to help you. Pamela M. Enlow, MSN, RN, author of "Coping With Anticipatory Grief," says overcoming depression helps us move beyond ourselves to heightened concern for the ill person. We focus on that person's quality of life.

Extreme Responses

In rare cases, people can develop illogical thinking. A woman who was preparing for her husband's death from Lou Gehrig's disease convinced herself that he had special after-death powers. After his death, she thought her husband would continue to watch over her, help with decision-making, protect her, and even change the weather. She continued to believe these things and mentioned them to friends.

This kind of thinking is bewildering, perhaps frightening, to family members and friends. Maybe you've had similar or odd thoughts. While this happens occasionally, you don't want to go on for a long time, and need to do something about it. **Contact a medical professional now if you are concerned about irrational thoughts.**

This chapter has examined some of the responses to early grief. Right now you are stumbling in the dark, tripping over stones, brambles, and twigs. Hard as it is to believe, the time will come when you round the bend, and see the end of the road. The end is really a beginning and these steps will lead you to it.

Healing Steps

- Find a safe retreat/refuge from distress and pain.
- Keep some social contacts.
- Get a physical exam if you haven't had one recently.
- Find ways to relax and detach.
- Get accurate information.
- Accept your anger and keep it from hurting others.
- Find an outlet for your emotions.
- Get answers to questions from someone you trust.
- Retain normal/pleasant activities without feeling guilty.
- Pace yourself and avoid doing too much.
- Be aware of your needs and meet them.
- Ask family members and friends to serve as reality checks.

- Learn to spot the symptoms of depression.
- Seek medical treatment if you're concerned about irrational thoughts.

CHAPTER 7
When Early Grief Gets Complicated

Grief can't be shared. Everyone carries it along, his own burden, his own way.

Anne Morrow Lindbergh

SMILING THROUGH YOUR TEARS: ANTICIPATING GRIEF

Early grief is complicated all by itself. As you go through the process you will face problems that complicate your grief even more. Family discord is one of these problems. You're entitled to your feelings and family members are entitled to theirs. However, some family members may have far different—even opposite—views than yours.

Sibling Rivalry

It is natural for siblings to want things that remind them of a loved one. A daughter may want her mother's dishes and a son may want his father's tools. Some family possessions may have special meaning for you. Problems may arise when siblings want the same things and start to argue. These arguments catch you off-guard, hurt the family, and hurt you.

Unresolved arguments may lead to permanent discord. Edward Myers, author of *When Parents Die*, says the root of discord may not be money, but sibling rivalry. He thinks one of the most common sore points between siblings is lack of cooperation during a crisis. Family members just can't get it together.

Other researchers share Myers' view. In their book, *Living Beyond Loss*, Froma Walsh and Monica McGoldrick say "longstanding sibling conflicts and cutoffs can often be traced back to the bedside of a dying parent." Similarly, it may be traced to the bedside of another family member or friend.

Now early grief is *really* complicated. Siblings may refuse to discuss care directives, settle unpaid bills, make burial arrangements, and take care of other unpleasant things. All they talk about is their "fair share" of the estate. Each family

member may have a different idea of what they should get. Before things get out of hand, **plan your responses to siblings.**
- Remember, early grief is a time of intense emotions.
- Think carefully before you speak.
- Stick to the present.
- Be willing to compromise.
- Ask your siblings to describe their emotional attachment to family items.
- Consider verbal promises when making decisions. Your loved one may have promised a family heirloom to a sibling or friend.
- Check written documents: wills, letters of intent, greeting cards, and e-mails.
- Sometimes loved ones write notes about their valuables. Look for notes tucked inside objects and/or taped to the bottom.
- Try to keep valuable collections in the family.
- Find an impartial mediator if necessary.

Now isn't the time to bring up long-standing disputes. Put these feelings aside for now. Time often changes things and you and your loved ones may see things differently later. Nothing replaces family, so do all you can to maintain good relationships. Years from now, if things don't go well, at least you know you tried.

Relationship Problems

Family problems may complicate early grief. One side of the family may hold a grudge against another side. These grudges may last for years. In fact, the original reason or reasons for the grudge may be forgotten. Yet the grudge persists and is passed on to children and grandchildren, hardly the best of legacies.

A poor relationship with your parents also complicates early grief. Parents and kids may have very opposite natures. A concerned daughter and her husband drove thousands of miles to help her ailing mother. "Norm worked on the outside of the house and I worked on the inside," she said. "Mother wasn't pleased with anything I did. I've been married for 40 years but she doesn't like the way I dust, scrub the floors, or make a bed. We argued the whole time I was there."

Though it is hard, **try to nurture family togetherness** during your early grief. Identify memories and plan events to promote family unity. Plan experiences that bring family members together, such as selecting photos to display at a memorial service, meaningful stories to tell, and the music that will be played.

Maintaining a marriage or relationship can be a problem for those who are going through early grief. Long-term caregiving leaves you little time to care for relationships. You and your partner may pass like two ships in the night. Understanding as your partner may be, you wish you had more time with him or her, and can't seem to find this time.

Nancy L. Mace and Peter V. Rabins, MD detail relationship problems in *The 36-Hour Day*. While they think good relationships can survive in the face of stress, they tell partners to talk to one another, get away, and "enjoy their relationship in the ways that they always have." Even if it means spending less time with your loved one, you need to **take care of your relationship.**

Dividing the Goods

Dividing the goods is such a problem the University of Minnesota developed a program called "Who Gets Grandma's Yellow Pie Plate?" It's one of the Extension Service's most popular programs. Shirley Barber, PhD, a member of the Extension Service staff, described the program at a 1999 meeting of the Minnesota Medical Association Alliance.

"Family objects transmit our family history," Barber said, "and that is why they are important." University of Minnesota researchers surveyed 75 families in preparation for developing the video and workbook. From the survey they identified six key factors (or themes) that apply to most families.

- Identify sensitive family issues.
- Determine what you want to accomplish.
- Decide what "fair" means in your family.
- Understand that items have different meanings to different people.
- Consider distribution options and the consequences of them.
- Agree to manage any conflicts that may arise.

Barber said it was a good idea to "put who gets what in writing." These stipulations may be cited in your loved one's will. Under Minnesota law, for example, a separate list may be made in conjunction with a will that lists items, descriptions of these items, and legal names of the people who are to receive them. The document must be signed, dated, and the ill person may wish to have it notarized.

Even with these preventive measures some pilfering may occur, according to Barber. So it's a good idea to **make a plan for dividing the goods** before your loved ones dies. Check state laws first. Then check legal documents: will, living will, Power of Attorney, and any other documents. Try to work out a fair system for dividing goods and property.

Still, your careful work may not be appreciated. One relative wanted his aunt's oil painting so badly that he went to her home while she was in the hospital and took if off the wall. Actions like these make relatives wince. These kinds of actions also turn family members into adversaries. Early grief doubles when a family member becomes your adversary. You grieve for a sick person *and* a sick family. Grieving for your family is like pouring salt on an open wound.

Lawyers are familiar with the infighting that goes on during early grief. Months from now you may be accused of taking advantage of the ill person and stealing things from the estate. If you have an adversarial relationship with a sibling you may wish to **protect yourself legally.** Legal protection saves you time, hassles, and may keep you out of court.

Protect Yourself Legally

Many who have gone through early and post-death grief have family horror stories to tell. "That won't happen to me," you say. "I have a wonderful, understanding family." This may be true. But stress often changes family relationships and, as a safety measure, you may wish to follow these tips from people who have completed early and post-death grief.

- Note your loved one's doctors appointments on a calendar.
- Keep track of the long-distance calls you make for your loved one.
- If you helped your loved one fill out his or her tax forms, save receipts, cancelled checks, and tax returns.
- Keep accurate financial records.
- Inventory your loved one's possessions and note special

items and/or collections. Give family members copies of the inventory.
- Provide family members with photocopies of medical and legal documents.
- Print-out e-mail communications that refer to setting the estate.
- Have a witness or witnesses on hand, if need be.
- Consult a lawyer.
- Leave an emotional door open because things could change.

While these tips may sound a bit harsh, it's better to be safe than sorry. Besides, the tips will help you track legal affairs and settle the estate after your loved one is gone. Settling the estate puts you face-to-face with death. So does the stigma of sexual disease. Stigma—the stain, reproach, and public criticism of your reputation and your family's reputation—makes the heavy burden of early grief even heavier.

Stigma of Disease

HIV/AIDS are global diseases and, though patients are living longer, there is a stigma associated with them. The HIV/AIDS patient lives with this stigma, his or her parents live with it, as do members of the extended family. Family members of AIDS patients are often blamed for the patient's disease. Vamik D. Volkan and Elizabeth Zintl describe this stigma in their book, *Life After Loss*. "An AIDS grief can resemble mourning a suicide in that the victim is blamed for his or her fate," they write. "Survivors get the message that their grief is less worthy of solace, so they not feel free to express their pain."

Social blame can force early grief inward. This is something you want to avoid. Stuffing away your feelings can lead to hidden sadness and anger. These emotions may emerge as depression or deep-seated anger, the kind of anger that affects everything you do.

Researcher Lori Wiener, PhD and her colleagues discuss the social implication of disease in their article, "The HIV-Infected Child: Parental Responses and Psychosocial Implications." Wiener and her colleagues conducted a descriptive study of parents whose children were in an HIV clinical trial. The purpose of their study was to understand early grief, anxiety, depression, and coping methods of the parents of infected children.

One hundred families participated in the eight-week study. Parents were examined by a Nurse Practitioner or Medical Doctor and demographic information was obtained. They were given various tests about anxiety, depression, coping, and early grief. The test results showed that parents of HIV/AIDS patients are more anxious than parents of children with other diseases.

One fourth of the parents surveyed had signs of moderate to severe depression. The age of the child also influenced parents' early grief. "As the child's age increased, so did anticipatory grief scores," the researchers report. The biological parents had more self-blame and early grief than adoptive parents. Parents must come to terms with the fact that the future they envisioned with their child may not happen, according to the researchers. Once their child becomes extremely ill and debilitated, "parents must begin to accept that the child will die." Wiener and her colleagues think their cross-sectional study points out a need for longitudinal studies.

Another study by Rebecca J. Walker, PhD and her colleagues examines the stigma of disease. They say AIDS/HIV has become more of a chronic disease and the stigma often spills over to the patient's family. This stigma interferes with the early grief process in many ways. Caregivers may see the AIDS/HIV patient as "less valuable" than others. Professional and family caregivers may keep the nature of the patient's problems secret. In an effort to be helpful some may try to rush these caregivers through early grief. As discussed earlier, well-meaning people may suggest developing new relationships before the patient has died.

Walker thinks the stigma of AIDS/HIV leads to hidden grievers. Shame, embarrassment, guilt and anger may cause caregivers (professional and family) to hide their grief. What's more, these caregivers may not seek support. And Walker points out that hiding grief drains energy from the grief work that has to be done.

Sometimes the stigma of hidden grief causes tension between the patient and caregiver. Plus, society may not approve the patient-caregiver relationship. The result is disenfranchised early grief—grief that can't be shown, validated, or displayed in public. **Share your feelings with health professionals** if a family member of friend has a sexually transmitted disease.

Many Losses

Though AIDS/HIV caregivers experience early grief, their many losses impede the process. Seeing the patient's physical changes—skin lesions, loss of stamina, memory problems, coordination and extreme weight loss—is devastating. You may feel like you have lost control of your relationship with the ill person and with your life. The degree of loss corresponds to your loved one's health.

Then, too, many of the patient's loved ones and friends may have died. These losses affect early grief because the griever moves quickly through the stages without completing them. Even if your loved one doesn't have AIDS, **try to**

complete each stage of grief as it comes. You may have to ask others to back off while you do this. Only you can decide what you need.

Sherry E. Showwalter, MSW refers to the complexity of grief in her article, "Walking With Grief: The Trail of Tears in a World of AIDS." She thinks the combination of many losses, broken spirits, loneliness, stress, depression, fatigue "and the possibility of community/family rejection" make early grief more confusing.

Chronic Grief

The parents of a chronically ill child live with the uncertainties of the disease every moment. Their chronic grief affects them, family members, and health professionals. Ralph C. Worthington, PhD describes this grief in "The Chronically Ill Child and Recurring Family Grief." He says chronic illnesses are incurable by definition, unless there is a technological breakthrough in the future. "Unlike the sequenced predictable stages of grief that families go through in facing terminal illness, the grief experienced by parents of the chronically ill is recurrent and cyclical," he writes.

Parents may grieve for the perfect child they didn't have. They may also grieve for the imperfect child they have and their child's medical treatment. In cases of spina bifida, for example, the child may need multiple corrective surgeries. Because of the child's uncertain life expectancy and/or quality of life, early grief increases.

Chronic illness makes huge demands on the family system. Family members may cope well at times and feel depressed, angry, and guilty at other times. Siblings may be jealous of the time and attention that the chronically ill child receives. Parents need to make a special effort to **help a healthy sibling or siblings.**

Try to find some one-on-one time with the other sibling(s) and participate in activity that promotes quality time together. Depending on your child's age, go to the playground, go swimming, or play a board game. While time is precious when you have an ill child, your other child or children need some special attention, too.

The parents of chronically ill children face another challenge—balancing life-saving measures with palliative care. Early grief may be acute during this time. Recently there has been more attention to providing hospice care and prescribing effective pain medication for seriously ill children. In the past some parents minimized the role of these approaches. They, and others, felt that the only important objective was to prolong a child's life even if the quality of life was poor and a cure was unexpected.

Avoiding Emotional Pain

Whether it is conscious or unconscious, we try to avoid emotional pain because it's a natural thing to do. But avoidance complicates early grief and sets us up for crisis. We must face our pain in order to recover, according to Judy Tatelbum, author of *The Courage to Grieve.* You may be afraid to do this because you think emotional pain will overcome you. "The only grief that does not end is the grief that has not been fully faced," says Tatelbaum.

Letting yourself feel emotional pain takes courage, courage you may not think you have. If you look deep inside yourself, though, you will probably find it. Facing emotional pain is something you do for yourself and helps you move beyond grief to a different life. Tatelbaum thinks grief needs attention—your attention—in order to heal.

Think of ways you can **face your emotional pain.** One way is to share it with family members. You may do this at a picnic, while fishing, walking along the golf course, or other times. Sharing your feelings will help you to see them more clearly and gauge their intensity. Other family members may benefit from your emotional honesty.

People who are going through early grief often benefit from a brief vacation. You may have to force yourself to take this vacation, but it's a good idea. This may be a good time to connect with nature because it's always changing, always wondrous, and eases your pain. Tuck images of nature in your mind and reflect on them.

Financial Worries

Add financial worries to early grief and you really have problems. Most medical costs are accrued at the end of the patient's life. Your loved one may have outstanding hospital bills, medication bills, private nursing bills, ambulance bills, and nursing home bills. Bills are all you think about. The family may not have enough money to cover these expenses. Talking to a social worker, hospital accounts officer, accountant or lawyer will help you to develop a plan.

Some families struggle with paying for care. Warren McCall detailed an Oregon family's struggle in an Associated Press article. An 18-year old cystic fibrosis patient, Brandy Stroeder, needed both a liver and lung transplant. Despite coverage under the Oregon Health Plan, her surgery was not approved, and without this surgery she would die.

Though Oregon pays for treatment, it pays according to a ranking system based on the medical odds for survival. "The best chances of recovery go to the top [of the list] and the worst chances drop to the bottom," McCall writes. Oregon Governor

John Kitzhaber, a former emergency room physician, said the case was a tragedy caused by the limitation of public resources. Brandy's parents went to court to overturn the state's decision.

We can only surmise Brandy's self-grief and her parents' early grief. An Associated Press photo shows Brandy in her hospital bed, an oxygen tube in her nose, and her mother's head pressed against her brow. A few weeks later a television newscast said a donor had come forth to pay for surgery. Few patients are as fortunate.

Medical bills can use up all of the family's resources. **Look into financial** assistance if you're worried about money. The funding is out there but you may have to search for it. "We thought we were going to pay all of the medical bills ourselves," said a concerned parent. "Then we found out we couldn't pay them and accepted help. I'm glad we did."

Resurrection-of-the-Dead Syndrome

With chronic and severe illnesses the patient may come close to death, only to recover. Charles David details this unusual process in his article "Resurrection-of-the-Dead Syndrome." He says the syndrome is characterized by a pattern of crisis and recovery, something that may happen to critically ill patients time and again. The syndrome is hard on everyone. "As a consequence of anticipatory grief the sick family member is perceived as 'not being alive' and is then treated as though he or she were dead," he explains.

Family members may start to talk about the ill person in the past tense. Just because your loved one is critically ill doesn't mean he or she is deaf. Hearing you talk this way makes your loved one feel worse. A loved one's miraculous recovery may result in emotional confusion for you and members of your extended family.

"My mother had been ill for years and I was trying to distance myself from her in preparation for her death," a son explained. "Mom looked like she was going to die at any minute. Then she recovered, woke up, and started asking about supper. I felt like I had been torn apart." Watch for the Resurrection-of-the-Dead Syndrome because it is an emotional roller coaster.

Decathexis

Decathexis is the process of distancing ourselves from a dying or deceased person. Therese A. Rando talks about the process in her book, *Grief, Dying and Death.* She thinks the single, most crucial task of grief is "untying the ties that bind us" to the deceased person. You may visualize the process as unclasping hands or fingers, according to Rando.

The deceased person isn't forgotten or betrayed, it's the nature of the relationship that has changed. "The relationship exists in a very special way in the heart and mind of the griever," she writes. Usually decathexis is a healthy approach, but withdrawing too soon from your loved one may harm that person and you.

So hang in there. If you are willing to stand the pain you may discover a beautiful light in the darkness of grief. One wife stayed with her husband from the first sign of illness until his last breath. They discovered the power of acceptance together, a power that she relies on today.

"My husband and I went [emotionally and spiritually] to a place that was so awesome," she said. "It was heartbreaking and extremely painful. I can't describe it, but it was awesome that we could do that together." At this dark time of life the couple felt closer than ever. This memory sustained the widow later.

Watch for signs of early decathexis. They include

things like cutting down your hospital visits drastically, not returning phone calls, and failing to do the errands you were supposed to do. You may find look for excuses not to contact with your loved one. As you process early grief be aware of the difference between decathexis and systemic decathexis.

Systemic Decathexis

Systemic decathexis is similar to decathexis, with one notable exception—it's a deliberate response. Elliott Rosen explains systemic decathexis in his article, "Families Facing Death." He thinks the grief process is not a linear one that can be defined by time and rigid stages. Instead, grief must be measured qualitatively.

Rosen thinks systemic decathexis is a qualitative experience because it includes the wishes of the dying person. "The tasks of grieving take on new dimensions when begun before rather than after death," he writes. Patients and family members may work together to make funeral and burial plans, or to create a lasting memorial for a loved one. Systemic decathexis shows that family members are emotionally intact.

Though they had never heard of systemic decathexis, Nelson and his younger brother worked on it together. Nelson was 82 years old, interested in life, an avid collector, and active in his condominium association. His activities stopped abruptly when Nelson was hospitalized for pneumonia. Worry about his antique vase collection kept Nelson from getting the rest he needed.

The collection was his pride and joy, the decorating feature of his condominium. What would happen to it? Nelson shared his worry with his younger brother. "I'll make arrangements for you," his brother said.

Much as they appreciated the collection, none of the other

condominium residents wanted the vases, even though they were free. Some residents worried about insurance costs. Others expressed concern about the fragility of the vases and having to dust them. Nelson was hurt by their lack of interest.

Then Nelson's brother contacted a local museum. The museum's director was delighted with the prospect of such a valuable donation and promised to display the vases in a special case. When he heard about the arrangements Nelson breathed a sigh of relief and died peacefully in his sleep a few weeks later. You may work on systemic decathexis by:

- creating a memory book with your loved one
- reviewing old photos and videos
- prepaying funeral arrangements
- writing your loved one's obituary
- cutting back on bedside visits (which may exhaust your loved one)
- arranging for donations to various charities
- sending health updates to relatives and friends
- planning a memorial service for your loved one

Though early grief may become complicated, you may find ways around these complications; it just takes time. You are the only person who can decide if you want to invest this time. These healing steps will help you develop more coping skills, the subject of the next chapter. Choose a step and start working on it now.

Healing Steps

- **Plan your responses to siblings.**
- **Nurture family togetherness.**
- **Take care of your marriage or relationship.**
- **Make a plan for dividing the goods.**
- **Protect yourself legally.**

- Share feelings with health professionals.
- Complete each stage of early grief as it comes.
- Help a healthy sibling or siblings.
- Face your emotional pain.
- Watch for the Resurrection-of-the-Dead Syndrome.
- Watch for signs of early decathexis.
- Plan your systemic decathexis.

CHAPTER 8
Adding to Your Coping Skills

One joy scatters a hundred griefs.

Chinese Proverb

SMILING THROUGH YOUR TEARS: ANTICIPATING GRIEF

This chapter is filled with practical coping tips. Notice that the title is *adding* to your coping skills, because you have some skills already. Yet there is no quick fix for early grief. You must find your own coping methods and do your own grief work. For most of us this work begins with crying, an upsetting response for you and those who care about you.

Does crying hinder or help you? Jeffrey A. Kottler, author of *The Language of Tears*, sees crying as a separate language system. Tears are one of the things that make us human, he says, and "crying is one of the things that bring us together." Despite differences in vocabulary, grammar, and accents, the language of tears crosses all geographical boundaries. Everyone cries and our tears show that we are emotionally moved.

Let Yourself Cry

If your tears are to have meaning they must enhance you in some way, according to Kottler. Crying releases pent-up emotions. You may cry a little or a lot or have bouts of crying, depending on where you are in the early grief process. Your tears communicate your feelings to others and, with some introspection, to yourself as well. Crying helps you to reach deep inside your soul.

Because crying is distracting, Kottler says you must pay careful attention to your thoughts while you're doing it. Listen to each thought as it enters your mind. Feel the tears trickle down your face. Hear your sniffles and sobs. Notice your body's other responses, too, such as gasping for breath or shivering. As you cry your thoughts may shift back to childhood. These links with the past may help you see the present more clearly and may pave the way for change. "Personal transformation is not only about thinking and feeling differently but also about behaving in new ways," says Kottler.

If you are to learn from early grief you need to **decode your personal language of tears**. What are your tears telling you? You may want to jot your thoughts down on paper. Some of your ideas may be conflicting or scary. Don't worry if you list contradictory feelings; time will help you to sort them out. Most likely you will have a mix of positive and negative emotions.

Reaching out to others is the last step of your transformation. You have many options here, everything from settling family arguments to volunteering at a nursing home. Let your tears lead you to new insights about people and life. All of this sounds good in theory, but what if you can't cry? Again, give yourself time. You may not be at that point in the early grief process yet.

What if you cry too much? Don't hold back the tears, but don't close yourself off either. Interact with your family and friends. Select some of the activities you enjoy and do them. Take the dog for a long walk, go to a concert with a friend, or spend time at an art museum. Getting away for an hour or so will make you feel better. This "recess" will also help you to cope with your feelings.

Your Approach to Coping

Men and women cope with problems differently and the differences in their styles are more pronounced during stressful times. Kimberley J. Chapman, BN, MSc and Carolyn Pepler, PhD, contrast male and female coping styles in their article, "Coping, Hope, and Anticipatory Grief in Family Members in Palliative Home Care."

SMILING THROUGH YOUR TEARS: ANTICIPATING GRIEF

Two main styles of coping—problem-focused and emotion-focused—had been reported in medical literature. Chapman and Pepler studied the relationship between these styles, hope, and early grief. Sixty-one family members (all over 18 years old) who had relatives in palliative care participated in the study. The family members took the non-death version of a grief experience inventory test (104 statements that comprise six bereavement scales) and other tests.

Results showed that women and young people used more emotion-focused coping than men. And because they were emotion-focused the women felt more despair, anger, and hostility. People who lived with the ill person used more confrontive [problem-based] coping strategies. Contrary to previous studies, the researchers found no relationship between education and choice of coping style. "It is possible that people who experience more anticipatory grief use more emotive coping strategies," say the researchers.

Determine your style and use it to your advantage. Make it work for you, not against you. If your style becomes too intense, tone it down and aim for middle emotional ground. Be aware of the impact of your coping style on others. Does your style encourage friends and family to offer support? Does it push them away? **Moderate your coping style if necessary.**

Stick to A Routine

You will function better if you **stick to your routine.** Think of routine as the backbone of your life, the support that keeps you standing and moving. Simple, repetitive tasks, such as making beds, washing dishes, and folding laundry, are comforting. While you are doing these tasks you can let your mind wander or do some serious thinking.

Sticking to a routine also gives you a sense of control over a life that is out of control. While you may not be able to stick to your entire routine, you may stick with parts of it. In other words, you adapt the routine to your needs. You may walk with your neighbors once a week instead of daily, for example. Trial and error will help you to fine-tune your routine.

Having a routine also helps the ill person. Your loved one may expect you to visit at certain times of the day and look forward to your visits. Doctors and nurses also have medical routines and your visits must coordinate with them. Of course, exceptions are made for patients who are critically ill and near death.

Routine is especially important for those with Alzheimer's disease, according to Nancy Mace and Peter Rabins, MD, authors of *The 36-Hour Day.* Having a routine makes them feel more secure and Alzheimer's patients may recall the routine despite their dementia. Routines that aren't working should be changed. You may wish to add journal writing to your routine.

Keep A Journal

Keeping a journal helps you to see the "big picture" of life and identify your needs. Your journal entries don't have to be long. Write your entries in a blank book, on the computer, or record them. Make sure you have given the date before you start recording. The method you use is less important than the journal process. Christina Baldwin describes the process in her book, *One to One: Self-Understanding Through Journal Writing.* She thinks journal writing helps us to let go.

"If you dialogued with grief, what do you think it would say to you?" she asks.

Answer this question now. Are there things you are hanging on to? If so, what is the value of keeping them? Do you need to let go of some things? Would letting help you in some way? Try to make regular, though not necessarily daily, entries in your journal. "When we grieve a loss, we create a space for fulfillment," Baldwin says.

Keeping a journal can help you to find this fulfillment. Here are some entries from the journal Harriet kept about her caregiving experiences with her mother. She kept the journal for almost a year and her entries give you a glimpse of the challenges Harriet faced. The entries also reveal her painful role reversal with her mother.

January 2nd

At lunchtime, Mom put her head in her hands and said she didn't know how she was going to get all the work done in preparation for moving [to a new community]. If nothing else, this Christmas has taught me that I am now the parent and Mom is now the child. Feeling depressed, I typed out a list for Mom, things to do, things to sell, things to keep. She has reread the list several times.

January 3rd

Since John gave me a new curling iron [for Christmas] I gave Mom my old one. It was touching—and heartbreaking—showing Mom how to use it. "I try to keep myself up," she said. I made several curls on each side of Mom's face. It was hard not to cry as I worked. Mom kept looking in the mirror, moving her head from side to side, and changing her stance. I looked too. Together we were Christmas past and Christmas future.

Other entries describe Harriet's sadness and vulnerability. Two years after her mother's death she read the journal. The entries describe one crisis after another and Harriet was shocked at what she had been through. But the most surprising thing was how the journal explained her needs. Harriet wished she had read the journal sooner.

Identify Your Needs

You need to figure out your needs during early grief. James W. Youll cites some of these needs in an article bout improving nursing care. He thinks our needs include spending time with a critically ill person, helping that person, getting more medical information, and getting emotional support. Chances are you also need some of the life essentials listed below.

- Well-balanced meals
- Adequate sleep
- More time for yourself
- More help from siblings
- Help with conveying health information to the ill person
- Help with conveying health information to family members
- Help with finding legal documents
- Medical-legal assistance
- Help with daily tasks, such as cleaning
- Transportation to and from the hospital
- Vacation from your problems

Companionship may be your greatest need, according to Judy Tatelbaum, author of *The Courage to Grieve*. She says, "We may need others to listen to us, to talk to us, to hold us, even to take over for us." Needs are a normal response when you're anticipating death. But Tatelbaum thinks your needs are greater if you handle them on your own and don't involve others. So it's wise to **identify your needs** as soon as possible. Once these needs are met identify your new ones. Keep on doing this throughout your early grief journey. Remember, observers may see your grief more clearly than you.

After visiting her critically ill son in the hospital, a grieving mother met a church friend in the hospital parking lot. The friend asked how the mother was faring in this time of crisis. "Oh, I'm getting along," she said. "But it's hard. I love to cook but I have no idea of what we're having for supper. We're almost out of groceries and I can't even make a list."

The friend went home and contacted members of the church caring committee. Homemade soups, stews, and casseroles were delivered to the mother's home the next day. On top of one casserole dish there was a note that read, "Don't bother to write a thank-you note. I wanted to do this for you." While the prepared food helped the couple to eat sensibly, the kindness of others helped them more.

Listen to the Sick and Dying

When you listen to the sick and dying, you show respect for life, not just the ill person's life, but your life, too. Listening helps you to discover things you may not have known. You may also discover things about yourself. Listening to the dying takes tremendous courage, and while you're doing it you must take care of yourself, according to Maggie Callanan and Patricia Kelly.

They offer some listening tips in their book, *Final Gifts: Understanding the Special Awareness, Needs, and Communication of the Dying.* You must pay close attention to the details of the conversation, the authors say, because conversations often contain important messages. While you don't want to force or push the conversation, you may ask questions. Phrase your questions in general terms and rephrase them for the hard of hearing. The ill person may ask you questions and you may choose to answer them or not. Only you can decide.

Andy's mother-in-law was in the hospital, dying from a rare form of cancer. Though his mother-in-law responded to doctors' and nurses' questions, she couldn't frame detailed answers or follow conversation. She was particularly confused about where she was and why she was in a strange place. "I didn't pack well for this trip," she told Andy.

It took Andy a few seconds to frame his reply. 'You're not on a trip, Mom," he said hesitantly. "You're in the hospital and you're very ill."

His mother-in-law stared intently at Andy. "That's a good thing to know, dear," she responded. Later that day Andy wondered if he should have been so honest with her mother-in-law. After some thought he decided that his honesty may have given her a clear, brief "window" in the midst of dementia. One week later his mother-in-law died.

Counseling

Grief counseling helps you to understand the grief process and grow from it. In her book, *Grief, Dying, and Death,* Therese A. Rando, PhD describes some counseling goals. Experts view these goals as interventions. Rando's list of goals is too long to include here, so we've selected just a few, and added some comments.

- Encourage the grieving person to cry. (This person may be you.)
- Encourage the grieving person to talk about their relationship with the ill or deceased person. (You may have to set aside time for this.)
- Provide the grieving person with information about the grief process. (Share this book with others, for example.)

- Help the grieving person to find ways of coping. (You may offer to get groceries or do other daily tasks.)
- Help the grieving person in finding ways to replenish himself or herself.
- Work with the grieving person to create—and invest emotionally—in a new life.
- Help the grieving person to see what he or she has derived from their loss. (This realization needs the perspective of time.)

Rando believes there are gains with every loss. "It is helpful for grievers to recognize gains and to capitalize on them in their recovery process," she writes. But you may not see these gains right now. Even worse, you may feel like you are emotionally stuck. Where do you go from here?

Some people who feel this way have benefited from guided imagery, a process done with the supervision of a trained therapist. Beatrice Turkoski, PhD, RN, and Brenda Lance, MSN,RN, write about guided imagery from a nursing perspective. They define guided imagery as a "therapeutic process by which patients are guided to harness their imagery—their mental imagining of positive events—such that they are able to communicate with the physiologic processes of the body outside of conscious awareness."

It's similar to daydreaming. The therapist guides you as images come into your mind, but all of the images are yours. Sometimes guided imagery includes envisioning a positive spiritual experience. Guided imagery has helped many, though it doesn't work for everyone. Experts say people who are strictly rational may not respond.

Guided imagery is done in a quiet room with dimmed lighting. The patient imagines scenes in his or her mind. The therapist helps the patient to develop these scenes by adding colors, sounds, smells, and other details. Each session lasts from 20-30 minutes. "Guided imagery can also be used to facilitate the process of 'letting go' for the patient and family," according to the researchers.

Consider grief counseling if you feel lost. For more information call your doctor, your local mental health agency, or a private psychological counseling group. As many grieving people have discovered, laughter may be just what the doctor ordered. You don't have to feel guilty for enjoying a good laugh during this sorrowful time.

Let Yourself Laugh

Just like tears, laughter makes us human. Laughter lifts our spirits and renews our energy. President Abraham Lincoln recognized this when he said, "With the fearful strain that is on me night and day, if I did not laugh I should die." Take a tip from President Lincoln and **look for laughter in each day.**

Your laughter also gives you a short break from your problems. Going out to lunch with close friends may give you the opportunity to laugh. You may laugh (though not very much) at a television comedy. No matter how bleak your life may seem, you still need to laugh. Lillian, the woman whose life was shattered by change, learned this at an odd time.

After her husband's memorial service Lillian stood in the receiving line and thanked guests for coming. Next in line was a close friend, who blurted, "I thought your life was lousy before, but this really sucks!" The comment was so outrageous that both women burst into laughter. "It felt so good to laugh," Lillian said. "I really needed that."

You may be able to find humor in odd situations like Ginny. Her husband was becoming increasingly demented. His waning social skills didn't prevent them from traveling and they went to Mount Rushmore National Park. They looked forward to the evening light show. Before the show Ginny's husband said he was going to the men's room. Only he didn't go to the men's room, he went to a food stand and bought a huge Coke in a souvenir cup.

"It was the largest size drink I had ever seen," Ginny recalled. "My husband was a thrifty man so it was rather funny to see him with this huge Coke."

Ginny wondered how he paid for the Coke because her husband had no money. The answer became clear when security guards approached her and said he had left the food stand without paying. "I paid them," she said. "After that happened I always went to the men's room with him and stood outside the door. It also made me realize that we couldn't go out among strangers any more."

Though the incident was painful, Ginny saw the humor in it, and it still makes her smile. Releasing your emotions with laughter may give you the courage to say what you are thinking. It also gives you opportunities to break "the conspiracy of silence." Unless they've been through it people don't understand early grief and we often suffer in silence.

Conspiracy of Silence

Researcher James W. Youll says keeping our thoughts to ourselves—silence—actually works against us. At first glance you might think silence protects medical staff, patients, and family members. It doesn't. "Silence is a false assurance that offers no emotional growth or understanding of the events which surround death and its finality," writes Youll.

Of course you want to keep some things to yourself, but you could talk about others. Several of the people who were interviewed for this book did so to break the conspiracy of silence. "I know it's going to be painful," a widower said, "but maybe someone will be helped." That is one reason for speaking out and the person who is helped may be *you*.

You may **break the conspiracy of silence.** Figure out when and how you will go about this. Chances are you have more options than you think. Read through this list. Find the option that suits you best now and act on it.

- Attend a church support group.
- Join an affinity group, such as the AARP group for widows and widowers.
- Attend hospital and hospice sessions.
- Volunteer in your community.
- Give talks about your loved one's disease and your early grief.
- Volunteer for national groups, such as the Make-A-Wish Foundation.
- Donate funds to national health organizations, such as the Alzheimer's Association.

Setting new goals may also help you to break the conspiracy of silence. Once you have decided on these goals you may wish to discuss them with family members and friends. At the very least, they may understand your goals and cheer you on. At the very most, they may help you to attain them. New goals are like the promise of spring.

New Goals

New goals don't have to be large, they can be as small as fixing breakfast for yourself. When you have achieved this goal, you set the next, and work through the day. Achieving small goals helps you to move on to larger ones. Some people who are going through early grief find it helpful to visualize scenes with their goals.

"All the time my husband was sick I continued to set new goals," a widow recalled. "I dreamed of opening a house where people in my same situation could stay, eat meals, and interact with people. I wanted to minister to them." This dream of a special, nurturing place continues to be one of her goals. She is also thinking about writing a book about her experiences.

A widower set new goals with the help of his dying wife. When she was in nursing care they discussed his future without her. First, she asked her husband to keep on working. The couple loved to travel (they had a storehouse of beautiful memories) and she asked him to keep on traveling. "She had no fear of dying," the husband recalled. "She just wanted to be pain-free. The thing that probably kept me going was her attitude. If I'm coping well today it's because of my wife."

Prioritize your goals after you have set them. Pamela M. Enlow, MSN, RN discusses priorities in her article, "Coping With Anticipatory Grief." Enlow thinks we must continue to set priorities despite our grief "no matter how undesirable they appear." Making the final preparations for your loved one's death may be priority one. This grief work is so painful and necessary that you may wish to ask for help.

Prepare

Your loved one may wish to join in the preparations to retain control over his or her life. A school nurse and her husband, who was dying of cancer, made all of the final preparations together. They purchased a cemetery plot, wrote the obituary, and selected his casket. "I know this sounds grim, but doing these things made us feel better," she said. "We wanted to spend every last minute together."

Do your preparation work. Start by reviewing what had been done and what needs to be done. Preparation work usually takes longer than expected so start early. Getting these things done will give you and your loved one some peace of mind.

- Gather legal documents together and store them in a safe deposit box.
- Photocopy legal documents.
- Get finances in order.
- Have plans for disbursement of non-titled property in writing.
- Encourage your loved one to give things away now. Items may be given to family members, collectors, groups, and museums.
- Make sure your loved one has a will.
- Check the wording of the will because laws may have changed.
- Have your loved one sign an organ donor document, if that is what she or he wants.
- Prepay the funeral expenses.
- Plan the memorial service.
- Write the obituary.
- Make a list of family members and friends to notify.

As you read through this list other preparations may come to mind. **Involve other family members in the preparation work.** This involvement will make them feel needed during this stressful time. Getting them involved now may also prevent misunderstandings later. One couple decided to sell their home and move into an assisted living facility. "My husband is very ill and Tall Pines has a nursing care unit. He will get better care there," his wife explained. "Neither of us want to move, but it's something you do for those you love."

Tap Spirituality

Remembering your religious and spiritual beliefs is another way of preparing. Elizabeth Kubler-Ross writes about the need for spiritual guidance in her book, *On Death and Dying*. She thinks relatives often deal with their agony alone. "It happens frequently that the relatives are sent from one person to the other and finally end up in the chaplain's office, not expecting many answers in regard to the patient but hoping to find some solace and understanding for their own agony."

Hospital chaplains and other clergy may help you to connect with a religious community. **Tap your religious and spiritual beliefs.** They may help you to see life in a larger, symbolic framework. Your belief system can nudge you away from grief and towards recovery. In his book, *Who Needs God,* Rabbi Harold Kushner says he worries about people who are willing to stay in the shadows. "I know how wrong it is, how unhealthy it is, to become one of those creatures who are comfortable only in the dark and gloom, who shrink from bright lights and laughter," he writes. Though he understands this kind of depression, Kushner thinks turning to religious beliefs is a better course of action.

As he waited for death, a husband and wife talked about their spiritual beliefs. God had a plan for them, they decided, and because it was God's plan they trusted God to see them through it. When she was walking along hospital corridors or sitting in the waiting room, the wife would look for distraught, anxious people. "My prayer would be, 'God, show me if there is someone here I could help,'" she said. She may helped many people just by listening to their stories. Faith helped her to heal after her husband's death and to make a new life for herself.

"Everything is new," she said with a smile. "Everything is a first."

Healing Steps

- Let yourself cry.
- Decode your personal language of tears.
- Determine if your coping style is emotion-focused or problem-focused.
- Moderate your coping style, if necessary.
- Stick to a routine.
- Keep a journal.
- Identify your needs.
- Consider grief counseling or guided imagery.
- Look for the laughter in each day.
- Break the conspiracy of silence.
- Set new goals.
- Do your preparation work.
- Involve family members in the preparation work.
- Tap your spirituality.

CHAPTER 9
How Early Grief May Help You

Life is what we make it,
always has been, always will be.

Grandma Moses

SMILING THROUGH YOUR TEARS: ANTICIPATING GRIEF

Early grief is a life-long process in response to various events. Painful as it is, some experts think the process may help you. Deborah Welch, RN, MSN discusses the benefits of early grief in her article, "Anticipatory Grief Reactions in Family Members of Adult Patients." She thinks early grief helps us to rehearse our emotions, a valuable life skill.

Rehearsing Your Emotions

Welch surveyed 41 family members of patients who had cancer. The participants took the Texas Inventory of Grief and other tests. Results showed that a family member's past experience with the death of an immediate family member from cancer was a determining factor in his or her grief responses. "It appears that the concept of emotional rehearsal may have had some positive effect on the degree of unresolved grief responses," she writes.

While you are absorbed in the drama of early grief, you are learning your lines for the post-death sequel. You are also learning your lines for future early grief experiences. Consider these emotional benefits.

Emotional rehearsal may make it easier to identify your emotions. Once you have experienced early grief, you are familiar with the feelings that come with it: confusion, denial, sadness, anger, depression, anxiety, and many opposite emotions. The next time around you may spot these emotions more quickly.

You may take protective measures. If you awaken to a dark, rainy morning, and the weather makes you feel down, you may call a friend to lift your spirits. You may take other protective measures, too, such as attending a support group meeting, talking with clergy, and visiting family members.

Rehearsing your emotions may help you to contain them. During rehearsal you may find ways to keep your emotions from ballooning. Instead of total confusion, you may have partial confusion. Containing your emotions, in some cases treating them, may prevent sad feelings from turning into depression.

You may discover which emotions are hardest for you. "I expected to feel sad and lost," a wife said. "But I didn't expect to feel constant anxiety. It gets worse and worse." Realizing that anxiety was difficult for her, she shared her feelings with family members and church friends. "I'm getting my support system in place," she told her husband, "because I know I'm going to need it."

Family members may be more understanding. Because they have seen your emotional rehearsal, they are familiar with your responses and coping methods. This dress rehearsal may help family members to understand—even predict—your behavior. Indeed, your rehearsal may become their rehearsal and help family members to cope with early grief.

Rehearsing your emotions may highlight the need for help. Families that are torn apart by conflict may benefit from coaching, according to Elliott Rosen, author of *Families Facing Death.* The purpose of coaching is to guide a person to change his or her position in the family system by addressing conflicts. While death may soon end the life of a loved one, Rosen says it doesn't have to end the life of a family.

Your may discover new coping methods. Early grief may cause you to think about things you haven't thought about before, such as a support system. Check your system now and fine-tune it if necessary.

Identify the people or groups you may turn to for support. Their support may range from attentive listening to help with problem solving, depending on your needs.

Apply your past early grief experiences to future ones. This will help to ease your anxiety. Turning to family members may help ease their anxiety as well. In times of trouble families can be kind, helpful, and wondrous support systems. Do you live close to your family members? Are you emotionally close to them?

Family Loyalty/Closeness

Family loyalty can be strong or fragile. Marilyn J. Mason discusses family loyalty in her book, *Making Our Lives Our Own.* She thinks there are two types of loyalty. One is natural, conscious loyalty, and the other is "invisible loyalty." You have probably experienced both types. Natural loyalty is based on genetics and the feelings you have for members of your immediate and extended family. Invisible loyalty is based on taught and/or learned behavior, or "unstated rules" as Mason calls them. These rules protect the family's tolerance for pain.

Family systems differ and the unstated rules in your family may help or hinder you. If members of your family tend to carry grudges, this unstated rule may work against you. Conversely, if your family is tolerant this unstated rule may work for you. Most families become closer during the early grief process. In his book, *Families Facing Death*, Eliott Rosen says early grief helps family members to tie up loose ends, resolve interpersonal conflicts, and say good-bye to a loved one. The ill person may participate in all of these tasks.

Indeed, the ill person may devote all of his or her energy to completing these tasks and others.

Early grief may be your last chance to document your

family's history. Your loved one may detail family stories, correct dates, or identify faces and places in photographs. Depending on your loved one's condition, your loved one may tape record stories or dictate them to you. Your loved one may give you historical documents, special letters, newspaper clippings and mementos for safekeeping.

Usually the families that are able to work through early grief are the healthy ones. The mutual respect family members have for one another allows them to voice opinions, have different opinions, and work out solutions. **Appreciate family loyalty and grow from it.** Your family members may be annoying at times, but they helped to make you who you are today. Keep this in mind when the going gets tough.

Reorganization

Reorganization is a benefit of early grief that isn't readily seen. Grief for a loved one may cause you to check practical things, such as a will and Power of Attorney. If the Power of Attorney is ill himself or herself, for example, then other legal arrangements will have to be made. You may wish to seek your lawyer's advice.

Researcher Elliott Rosen talks about the reorganization that has to be done. "The reorganization that must take place in the family can begin in the presence and with input from the dying family member," he writes. Early grief gets reorganization in motion, according to Rosen. What kinds of reorganization is he talking about?

The ill person may begin to meet frequently with family members. In one case, Rosen said a terminally ill mother and her daughters planned holiday celebrations together. The mother asked her children to maintain this family tradition after her death. Rosen thinks experiences like these show that early grief involves interaction and purposeful planning.

Reorganization also leads families to think about a future without their loved one. These families are reinvesting in the future, according to Rosen. Are you reinvesting in the future? You may decide to sell a car or investigate retirement communities in your state or other states. One couple reviewed financial arrangements in preparation for the husband's forthcoming surgery.

"We're organized people, so we thought we had our ducks in a row," the wife explained. "It turns out our ducks weren't in a row and some legal documents were missing. We had to talk with our lawyer again. I'm glad we had this drill."

Reorganization is added pain to the pain you already feel. Yet it is necessary. The experience may draw you even closer to a loved one. **Take steps to reorganize your life** because it can be a fulfilling process for your loved one and family members. Bit by bit, and with steady effort, you will get the reorganization jobs done.

Empathy

Empathy is the realization and understanding of another person's feelings, needs, and suffering. Early grief may make you a more empathetic person, according to Marilyn J. Mason, PhD. She sees empathy as a "healthy joining, a healthy dependency we work *with*, not against." Mason has come up with a dozen "growth-enhancing" rules for mutual empathy.

The stipulations of rule 11 are an example: "I promise to respect and have compassion for your struggle as well as mine." Mason thinks rules like these demonstrate our caring for others. Perhaps early grief has caused you to think of similar rules.

"My early grief taught me a lot," a grandmother said. "Now I'm more aware of people who are in emotional pain.

I can tell by their eyes and body language and conversation. When I talk with them I try to make them smile. If nothing else, I listen." This approach doesn't make her an amateur therapist, she added, but it does make her a better human being.

Show your empathy for others. Be honest about your feelings and offer to help in any way you can. The smallest kindness, such as making a phone call, may be extremely helpful. You may show empathy for others by delivering flowers to a nursing home. Think of ways to show your empathy now. Showing your empathy helps you to see—and understand—the sacredness of life.

Appreciation of Community Services

Sooner or later, the early grief journey leads you to community services. Though you are aware of community services you may have not used them before. "I had no idea Social Services did so much!" a family caregiver exclaimed. "They gave me sound advice and I followed it." In discovering community services she discovered a new community.

September 11th made Americans grateful for the support they received from firefighters, policemen, emergency medical teams, Red Cross volunteers, chaplains, grief counselors and countless others who put their lives on the line. The heroic efforts of the firemen, those who lived and those who died, made Americans weep. The camaraderie of the policemen made us weep more.

As a nation we became more aware of community support. Kids sent letters of thanks to local firemen and policemen. Terrorism has given us a renewed appreciation of community workers. In addition, it has given us a renewed appreciation of freedom. Let us hold these thoughts in our hearts as we face the years ahead.

SMILING THROUGH YOUR TEARS: ANTICIPATING GRIEF

Death is Part of Life

Viewing death as part of life is a harsh reality to accept. We must also accept that fact that there is such a thing as "appropriate death." Health professionals use the term to describe a broad program of care. Avery D. Weisman, MD details this program in his article, "Appropriate Death and the Hospice Program." He defines appropriate death as a program that coordinates good coping skills with the reality of inevitable death.

"Appropriate death is a focus for hospice programs," he says, "regardless of their format and size of staff." There are three key parts to the hospice program: appropriate death for patients, early grief work and counseling, and maintaining caregivers' morale. Caregivers try to provide the best medical, nursing, and psychosocial care. Weisman says there are leading criteria for an appropriate death, all beginning with the letter c.

Care refers to total care, including pain relief, control of nausea, and other debilitating symptoms. If your loved one isn't receiving this kind of care a patient advocate may be of help.

Control refers to the patient's participation in a treatment plan, self-care, and crucial decisions. You want your loved one to feel like he or she still has some control over life.

Communication refers to interactions between hospital staff, patient-caregiver communication, and family communication. A patient communicator and social worker can help to keep communication flowing.

Composure refers to keeping moods and emotions within bounds. However, this is sorrowful work and you shouldn't expect your loved one's self-grief or your early grief to disappear.

Continuity refers medical treatment and protection of the patient's identity during the last stages of life. In some instances, hospital staff may give the patient a pseudonym to protect his or her identity.

Closure refers to the dying person's recognition of the end of life. Your spiritual advisor or the hospital chaplain may be extremely helpful at this time.

If you have had personal experience with illness, such as breast cancer, you know you are not invincible. You know you're not going to live forever. As you cope, **try to view death as part of life.** Early grief may help you to figure out what is really important to you. In fact, you may rethink what is important to you, your children, your grandchildren, and your extended family. Old ideas may be replaced with new ones.

What's Important?

Journalist Betty Rollin, in a television interview on "Quiet Triumphs," put it bluntly. "Cancer survivors are such a merry group," she said. "We know we might have croaked." Rollin believes cancer improved her life by keeping her on track.

Similarly, if you have been through early grief before, or self grief like Rollin, you know what is important. "Family comes first," according to one husband. "I am proud of my children and grandchildren. And I am grateful to still have meaningful work. The older I get, the more I value simple things—a roof over my head, a warm house, nourishing food, and a comfortable couch. I don't take any of these things for granted."

During a crisis little things fall away from your life like brown leaves from a tree. After the leaves are gone you see the trunk of the tree, its branches, and maybe even some roots. These are the tree's supporting structure. The important things in your life are your supporting structure. **Figure out what is important to you.**

At this moment, helping your loved one may be most important. When you love someone you invest your emotions in that person. This is called cathexis. To visualize this connection grief expert Therese A. Rando, PhD asks people to clasp their hands together as if they were praying. Your interlocking fingers represent the emotional bonds of your relationship.

Life changed in an instant with the terrorist attacks on the World Trade Center, the Pentagon, and the plane crash in Pennsylvania. Things that had been important before suddenly became trivial. Americans focused on the things they cared about most, sorrow for the innocent people who were killed, and appreciation of family and country. What do you care about most?

Death may change your active relationship with a loved one, but it doesn't change the emotional bonds that you feel. You may remember these bonds for the rest of your days. Knowing what is important may also help you to live each day. Once you have learned to appreciate each day you may go on to appreciate each moment.

Live the Moment

None of us know how long we will live. We don't know how long our loved one will live, either. Because we don't know these things, we may as well focus on what we do know. Each morning we awaken to a new day. We have the mental power to make this day joyous or sorrowful. Her Majesty Queen Noor of Jordan talked about the challenge of living the day on the "Larry King Live" television program.

She described King Hussein's battle with cancer and its impact on both of them. "Cancer defined every moment of our lives for all those months we were in hospital," she explained.

While he was ill, the king and queen visited other cancer patients, and met with cancer survivors. Sometimes King Hussein was allowed to leave the hospital. What did the king and queen do? They rented a Volkswagen beetle and drove to Iowa, where they purchased some Amish quilts.

During her husband's illness, treatment, and remission, Queen Noor didn't let early grief get the best of her. "You attune yourself to a very spiritual level when you are fighting cancer," she said. Queen Noor talked freely about the spiritual connection she feels with her deceased husband and her plans for continuing the work they started together. "Each moment of life is a miracle," she said.

Though you are sad, bewildered and hurting, **enjoy the miracle of the moment.** This doesn't happen automatically, you have to work at it. You have to make a conscious decision to be positive. This decision influences more than your day or week, it influences your view of life. Mayo Clinic Chaplain Warren Anderson sees grief as awful and *awe-full.* In an article called "Grief Process a Continuum" Anderson says our contact with grief [early and post-death] gives us a deeper appreciation of life. "Grief opens up our world and gives us wisdom we would not have."

Like Anderson, you may see grief as awful and awe-full. Certainly, you know more about early grief now than when you began this book. Even with this information you may have to struggle to enjoy the moment. The ability to enjoy the moment gets easier with practice. These ideas will get you started and you'll probably think of others.

- Turn off the television/radio/stereo while eating.
- Eat your meals slowly and savor every bite of food.
- Give yourself at least 15 minutes of silence per day.
- Make physical activity part of every day.

- Meditate regularly and/or connect with spirituality.
- Surround yourself with life—flowering plants, pets, and children.
- Do thoughtful things for other people.
- Create something: bake bread, paint a picture, knit a scarf, or do other things that interest you.

Maria had been interested in art since she was a child. She was an art minor in college and earned a Master's degree in art. Throughout life, when she was restless or sad, Maria turned to art for solace. When her husband developed chronic illness she discovered a new project, making mosaic flower pots. Maria created the mosaics from chipped antique plates.

"Did you ever wonder why you are whacking plates with a hammer at this stage of your life?" a friend asked.

"No," she replied. "But now that you mention it I understand it. Making flowerpots is a wonderful way to handle early grief. I look for plates in antique stores and every trip is a treasure hunt. Breaking the plates relieves my anger and then I create something beautiful." After hearing Maria's reply her friend asked how to make mosaic flower pots.

Shorter Post-Death Grief

Grief experts, including Elizabeth Kubler-Ross, think early grief shortens post-death grief. "The more this grief can be expressed before death, the less unbearable it becomes afterward," she writes. Many people who have completed early and post-death grief agree with this premise.

Robert Fulton, PhD agrees with this theory. In his article, "The Many Faces of Grief," Fulton says the "anticipation of death has allowed for the discharge of feelings prior to death and has obviated behaviors that one would normally expect." But other researchers disagree with Fulton and Kubler-Ross and see no value in early grief. Who is right? Researchers would have to interview hundreds of people to answer this question.

Many who have completed early grief, however, believe it shortened their post-death grief.

For eight years Jayne grieved for her ailing husband, who contracted several chronic diseases. With each disease his mental acuity decreased. Over time, it decreased to the point where her husband sat in a chair and recited nursery rhymes. "In my mind he died then," Jayne said. "When he really died I was grieved out because I had done my grieving beforehand."

Just as each person is different each grief experience is different. Therese A. Rando, PhD, in her book *Grief, Dying and Death*, says early grief may decrease abnormal grief. So there may be that benefit as well. Until you have completed the entire grief process you won't know if early grief helped you.

Still, if you accept early grief and don't fight it, you may reap benefits. **Be open to the idea that early grief shortens post-death grief.** It's worth a try. Your hopeful attitude will help you to make something good out of grief. In order to do this, you may wish to consider your loved one's occupation, interests, hobbies, and causes.

Good From Grief

Lance and Jenny grieved for their daughter for years. Early in life their daughter had developed diabetes and, despite the latest medical treatment, the disease became worse. The gradual loss of sight forced their daughter to curtail her activities. Though her parents, siblings, and friends thought the young woman would die from diabetes, she was killed in a car crash.

The couple handled their loss in an unusual way. In

memory of their beloved daughter they published a diabetes textbook and gave a copy to every incoming student at the local medical school. Others have created beautiful things from the darkness of grief.

When her mother was close to death a grieving daughter started a garden in memory of her mother. She worked in the garden almost every day, tilling soil, pulling weeds, and planting flowers. After her mother's death the garden became larger, with winding paths, wooden benches, bird feeders, and an amazing variety of plants. "I didn't realize this garden was for my mother until she died," the daughter said.

A few years later the daughter moved to a different home. Friends couldn't understand how she could leave her beautiful garden. The daughter, who also worried about leaving the garden, came up with an ingenious solution. She dug up some of her favorite plants, including ones that friends had given her, and transplanted them in a new memory garden. The new garden is even more beautiful than the old.

Creating something positive from negative feelings is a way of coping. Pesach Krauss and Morrie Goldfischer discuss coping in their book, *Why Me? Coping With Grief, Loss and Change.* They think we need to shift our focus from a direct relationship with shared values to a different kind of relationship with our loved ones. "In that way we free ourselves from the cold grip of the past to embrace warm and tender memories and action for the present."

Make something good from grief. Donate research funds or create a special memorial. Brainstorm about this and you will probably come up with lots of ideas. Some families have made patchwork quilts from their loved one's garments. Giving hope to others is another way to make something good out of grief.

Matthew Stolle described a cancer survivor celebration in Rochester, MN in his *Post-Bulletin* article, "Giving Hope to Others." The celebration was a cooperative effort between Mayo Clinic and the American Cancer Society. Cancer survivors were invited to a picnic that included music, games, prizes, balloons and lots of good food. But the main focus of the picnic was the banner that cancer survivors signed.

The banner was for Mayo Clinic's Oncology department. Mary Burk, a Mayo Clinic nurse, said the banner would inspire newly diagnosed patients. "They'll see [cancer survivors] of 20 years and 50 years and it inspires hope," she said. Offering hope to others may lead you to your own healing path, a journey that takes you from pain to joy.

Your Healing Path

Pesach Krauss and Morrie Goldfischer, authors of *Why Me? Coping With Grief, Loss and Change*, think grief helps us to heal the painful hurts in our lives. Early grief may cause you to think about your loved one's values. One grieving daughter recalled her father's generosity. "Our family didn't have much money," she said, "but my father always gave money to our church and to family members in need. He was a kind person." The daughter found comfort in this memory and she vowed to continue her father's kindness.

Her decision proved to be a giant step on her healing path. **Find your healing path.** Create it from the pain you feel, the love you feel, and decide where you want it to go. Along the way, you may rediscover the joy of simple things like sunshine and rain. An appreciation of life's simple gifts may evolve into a deeper appreciation of life and the various paths in your life, including the one you are walking now.

Your healing path may become a life path. In *Wisdomkeepers,* a book about Native American spirituality, medicine man Charlie Knight says the Ute have different songs for different things in their lives. The songs are a musical history of the Ute people and Knight sings them to a drum accompaniment. "Everyone has a song," he explains. "God gives us each a song. That's how we know who we are."

Early grief may help you discover who you really are—your true identity. You may evolve into a new person, someone you didn't know before, and would like to know better. Your loved one wouldn't want you to grieve forever so get out, do things, and help others. Create your own life song. Sing joyfully, in as true and clear a voice as you can find. If only one person hears your song that is enough.

Healing Steps

- Apply past early grief experiences to future ones.
- Savor family closeness and loyalty.
- Take steps to reorganize your life.
- Show your empathy for others.
- Try to view death as part of life.
- Figure out what is important to you.
- Enjoy the miracle of the moment.
- Be open to the idea that early grief shortens post-death grief.
- Make something good from grief.
- Find your healing path.

CONCLUSION

How amazing it is to be alive!
Anyone who lives and breathes and puts both feet on the ground,
What possible reason could he have for envying the Gods?

Paul Claudel, 1890

SMILING THROUGH YOUR TEARS: ANTICIPATING GRIEF

This book has focused on the early grief from start to finish. The Healing Steps within its pages lead you to your healing path. Whether your path is short or long, keep walking until you reach the end. If you haven't found your path yet don't worry. Your path will become clearer in time, for time really does heal wounds.

We wrote the book to help you understand early grief, but it doesn't exempt you from the process. Early grief is part of life and your experiences with it will be with you forever. Television and print news reports are filled with early grief stories, though we may not recognize them as such. "Endless Shock" is the title of one newspaper article.

It tells about a University of Wisconsin student, Michael Noll, who went missing after celebrating his birthday with college friends at a local bar. Despite the efforts of volunteers, body-detecting dogs, family members, and friends, the student was never found. A related article reported that Noll's family was "in endless shock."

In a second related article Kent Pederson, a friend of the missing student, says, "There's an entire world that isn't as connected to this." The problem isn't that people are uncaring, according to Pederson, the problem is that people don't understand [early grief]. "They don't know about this." Pederson unknowingly pinpointed one of the main reasons we wrote the book.

Until the end comes early grief is ongoing shock. Most people don't know about early grief and therefore don't understand it. Public understanding of early grief is minimal, at best, though things are starting to change. We believe people need to know about this kind of grief, learn to recognize it, and develop ways of coping. Further study on early grief is also needed.

Rebecca J. Walker and her colleagues ask for more research on the benefits of early grief in their article "Anticipatory Grief and AIDS." They say the research on early grief has been inconclusive as to whether it reduces the length of post-death grief. Walker isn't the only one asking for more study on early grief.

Kimberley J. Chapman, BN, M. SC, and Carolyn Pepler, N, PhD think more research is needed on early grief patterns within families. "The relationship between age and relation to family member needs to be explores further with adolescents and children," they write. Early grief touches children in ways we may not see or understand and we need to know more about these ways in order to help them.

Grahm Fulton and his colleagues, authors of "The Social Construction of Anticipatory Grief," think early grief needs to be examined from a social viewpoint. They see a need for more information about a terminally ill patient's grief (called self-grief in this book) and believe it would help the dying. This knowledge would also be helpful to medical professionals.

Fulton and his colleagues also see a need for more information on the emotional responses to early grief. They think it's "important for research to examine how the future is conceptualised by individuals and professional health careers." Since words can be confusing they recommend a qualitative approach to research, one that allows people to express ideas in their own words.

There is also a need for research on the cultural responses to early grief. No matter where we live, how we look, what language we speak, how we dress, or how we behave, early grief is common to human experience. We all want the same things: water, food, clothing, shelter, transportation, fulfilling work, fair wages, and time for fun. Most of all, we want our children and grandchildren to be happy.

Writing this book pointed out the need for more support services. People who are in the throes of early grief need a variety of services and they need them fast. Phone numbers, fax numbers, and e-mail numbers for these services should be readily available. It would be helpful if Web sites had "hot buttons" that link people to early grief support.

Early grief touches us all and we get through it by connecting with one another. Perhaps the British poet John Donne says it best in his poem, "For Whom the Bell Tolls." The poem begins with the line, "No man is an island, entire of itself." Donne goes on to say we are part of the main and share each other's joys and sorrows. You don't have to be alone on your island of early grief. Reach out to others and deep inside yourself. The human spirit is resilient. You may smile through your tears and, from the ashes of early grief, create a new and meaningful life.

APPENDIX A
Words to Know

adaptational tasks tasks a family member/caregiver needs to complete before the death of their loved one

affinity group a group with similar goals and interests, such as Alcoholics Anonymous

agitation extreme restlessness and nervousness

adjustment pattern changes in behavior and activities in order to solve problems and meet needs

anger an acute emotional reaction caused by a variety of situations; a common response to anticipatory and post-death grief

anniversary reaction renewed anticipatory or post-death grief prompted by special dates and/or events

anticipatory grief feelings of loss before a death or dreaded event occurs

cathexis emotional investment in another person

chronic grief recurring anticipatory grief of family members in response to the chronic illness of a loved one

coaching the process of guiding a person to change his or her position in the family by addressing/facing conflicts

decathexis emotional withdrawl from a dying or deceased person

delayed grief pushing aside feelings in order to deal with pressing needs

denial the unconscious process of allowing your thoughts to drift to other topics

depression pessimistic view of events and the future which lasts at least for weeks; depression is *not* "the blues"

detachment lack of involvement with other people; the ability to remove yourself mentally from a situation; tendency to view your own problems objectively/unemotionally

displacement transference of emotional attachment to a proper substitute

early grief another term for anticipatory grief

emotional limbo feeling caught in an uncertain state and/or being unsure of how you feel or how to behave

empathy realization and understanding of another person's feelings, needs, and suffering

family system general methods of operating and reacting within a family and an extended family

flat affect no expression of feelings, caused by emotional overload and stress

grief history the cumulative grief experiences in a person's life

grief triggers incidents and events that cause you to recall your feelings of anticipatory and post-death grief

grief work conscious efforts to handle/process anticipatory and post-death grief

guided imagery a therapeutic process that helps people to harness and use their mental images of events; training in self-regulation

hidden grievers family members who conceal their early grief due to shame, embarassment, guilt, or anger

SMILING THROUGH YOUR TEARS: ANTICIPATING GRIEF

hyper behavior excessive activity to avoid confronting painful thoughts

living-dying interval time between expected death and actual death

palliative end of life care; medical treatment to reduce the effects of illness

panic response abrupt intense anxiety

personality an enduring pattern of traits that make each person unique

post-death grief the grief process after a loved one, friend, or pet has died; post-death grief follows anticipatory grief

psychiatrist a medical doctor with additional training in mental health

psychologist a professional with training in human behavior/responses who may or may not have a state license to see patients

reality check evaluating whether perceptions mirror real events

Resurrection-of-the-Dead syndrome a pattern of medical crisis, followed by the patient's surprising recovery

surrogate griever health professionals' grief for the patients they are treating

sublimation redirecting socially unacceptable impulses into acceptable channels

support system people who provide emotional assistance

supression voluntary inhibition of activities and ideas

uncompleted loss loss that is not yet final

systemic decathexis planned emotional withdrawl from the dying person and the ability to envision a future without that person

APPENDIX B
More Reading

American Red Cross. "Facing Fear: Helping Young People Deal With Terrorism and Tragic Events" brochure, no date.

American Red Cross. "Your Family Disaster Plan" brochure, September 1991.

American Red Cross Disaster Services. "Helping Young Children Cope With Trauma" brochure, September 2001.

American Red Cross Disaster Services. "How Do I Deal With My Feelings?" handout, no date.

American Red Cross Disaster Services. "How You Can Help Yourself and Others" handout, no date.

American Red Cross Disaster Services. "Why Do I Feel Like This?" brochure, September 2001.

Baldwin, Christina. *One To One: Self Understanding Through Journal Writing.* New York: M. Evans and Company, Inc., 1997, pp. 148-156.

Barber, Shirley, PhD. "Who Gets Grandma's Yellow Pie Plate?" presentation, Minnesota Medical Association Alliance, March 19, 1999.

Braiker, Harriet B., PhD. *Getting Up When You're Feeling Down.* New York: Pocket Books, 1988, p. 186.

Buckman, Dr. Robert. *"I Don't Know What to Say": How to Help and Support Someone Who is Dying.* Boston: Little, Brown and Company, 1989, pp. 22, 88, 141.

Callanan, Maggie and Kelly, Patricia. *Final Gifts: Understanding the Special Awareness, Needs, and Communication of the Dying.* New York: Bantam Books, 1993, pp. 2-3, 241-242.

Caruso-Herman, Dorothy. "Concerns for the Dying Patient and Family," *Seminars in Oncology Nursing*, Volume 5, No. 2, pp. 120-123, 1989.

Chapman, Kimberly J., BN, MSc and Pepler, Carolyn, N., PhD. "Coping, Hope, and Anticipatory Grief in Family Members in Palliative Home Care," *Cancer Nursing*, Volume 21, 1998, pp. 226-233.

Children's Hospital Boston, "Child Health A to Z: Anticipatory Grief," www.Childrenshospital.org/cfapps/A...picDisplay.cfm?Topic=Anticipatory%20Grief

David, Charles J., MB, DPM, FRCP. "The Resurrection-of-the-Dead Syndrome," *American Journal of Psychotherapy*, January 1980, pp. 119-127.

Duke, Susan, MSc, BSc (Hons) RGN, PGDE, RNT. "An Exploration of Anticipatory Grief: the Lived Experience of People During Their Spouses' Terminal Illness and in Bereavement," *Issues and Innovations in Nursing Practice*, Volume 28, 1998, pp. 829-839.

Enlow, Pamela M., MSN, RN. "Coping with Anticipatory Grief," *Journal of Gerontological Nursing*, July 1989, pp. 36-37.

Fulton, Graham, et al. "The Social Reconstruction of Anticipatory Grief," *Social Science Medicine*, Great Britain, 1996, pp. 1349-1357.

Fulton, Robert, PhD and Bendiksen, Robert, PhD, editors. *Death & Identity*. Philadelphia: The Charles Press, 1994, pp. 168-174, 177-209, 247.

Gola, Hank. "Payton Awaits a Liver," *New York Daily News* article published in the *Post-Bulletin*, February 3, 1999, p. 1A.

Grams, Senator Rod. "Concern on Drug Issues Comes From Family Experience," *Post-Bulletin*, November 24, 1999, p. 11A.

Gyulay, Jo-Eileen, RN, PhD. "Grief Responses," *Issues in Comprehensive Pediatric Nursing*, December 1989, pp. 1-31.

Hodgson, Harriet. "Grieving Process a Continuum," *Post-Bulletin* Special Insert, September 14, 1998, p. 10.

Huber, Ruth, PhD and Gibson, John W., DSW. "New Evidence for Anticipatory Grief," *The Hospice Journal*, volume 9, 1990, pp. 49-67.

Jones, Alun, RMN, RGN, DipN, CPNCert. "Actors in an Emotional Drama: Inter-related Grief in Terminal Care," *Professional Nurse,* July 1992, pp. 598-603.

Jones, Patricia S. PhD and Martinson, Ida M. PhD. "The Experience of Bereavement in Caregivers of Family Members with Alzheimer's Disease." *IMAGE: Journal of Nursing Scholarship*, Volume 24, Number 3, Fall 1992, pp. 172-176.

Jowsey, Sheila, MD. "Mayo Clinic Office Visit: Coping With Bioterrorism," *Supplement to Mayo Clinic Women's HealthSource*, January 2002.

Kennedy, Dan. "Coping with Loss: Teachings of a Master," *World: The Journal of the Unitarian Universalist Association*, July/August 2000, pp. 19.

Kerr, Rita Butchko, RN, PhD. "Meanings Adult Daughters Attach to a Parent's Death," *Western Journal of Nursing Research*, August 1994, pp. 347-360.

Kissane, David W. et al. "Family Grief Therapy: A Preliminary Account of a New Model to Promote Healthy Family

Functioning During Palliative Care and Bereavement," *Psycho-Oncology*, volume 7, 1998, pp. 14-25.

Kottler, Jeffrey A. *The Language of Tears.* San Francisco: Jossey-Bass Publishers, 1996, pp. 1, 72, 168-184, 187.

Krauss, Pesach and Goldfischer, Morrie. *Why Me? Coping With Grief, Loss, and Change.* New York: Bantam Books, 1990, pp. 59, 130-139.

Kubler-Ross, Elizabeth. *On Death and Dying.* New York: Collier Books, Macmillan Publishing Company, 1969, pp. 4, 140-142, 147, 149-150.

Kushner, Rabbi Harold. *Who Needs God.* New York: Bantam Books, 1989, pp. 30-31, 106, 175-176.

LeSure, Elizabeth. "Families Struggle to Keep Hope Alive," Associated Press article published in the *Post-Bulletin*, September 14, 2001, p. 4A.

Lynch, Joshua. "Endless Shock: Friends, Coworkers Help Look for Missing Rochester Man," *Post-Bulletin*, November 18, 2002, p. 1A.

Lynch, Joshua. "Wed in a Week," *Post-Bulletin*, March 10, 2003, p. 1A.

Lynch, Joshua. "Friends Keep Hope Alive During Search," *Post-Bulletin*, November 18, 2002, p. 3A.

McCall, William. "Oregon Family Battles State Over Multiple Transplant," Associated Press article published in the *Post-Bulletin*, June 10, 2000.

McIver, Mary. "Healing the Hurt: How do You Explain the Death of a Loved One to a Young Child When Your Own

Heart is Torn Apart," *First Magazine*, May 22, 1995, pp. 87-89.

Mace, Nancy L. and Rabins, Peter V., MD. *The 36-Hour Day*. New York: Warner Books, 1981, pp. 33, 214.

Mason, Marilyn J., PhD. *Making Our Lives Our Own: A Woman's Guide to the Six Challenges of Personal Change*. San Francisco: HarperSanFrancisco, 1985, pp. 23, 42-43, 98-100, 109-124, 209.

Myers, Edward. *When Parents Die: A Guide for Adults*. New York: Penguin Books, 1987, pp. 47-50, 83, 88-89, 94, 101, 117.

National Alliance for the Mentally Ill (NAMI), "For Parents—A Depression Checklist," www.nami.org/youth/checklist.html.

National Association of School Psychologists. "A National Tragedy: Helping Children Cope—Tips for Parents and Teachers," www.nasponline.org/NEAT/terrorism.html.

Ode, Kim. "Worse, Best of Times: Sometimes, It Takes Tragedy to Bring Out the Finer Things in the People Around Us," *Star-Tribune*, January 18, 2004, p. E2.

Osterholm, Michael, PhD, MPH. "Bioterrorism: The Next Chapter." Presentation to the Minnesota Medical Association Alliance, September 19, 2002, Radisson Metrodome Hotel, Minneapolis, MN.

Osterweis, Marian, Solomon, Fredric, and Green, Morris, Editors. *Bereavement: Reactions, Consequences, and Care*. Washington, DC: National Academy Press, 1984, p. 49.

Queen Noor of Jordan, "Larry King Live" television program, June 24, 1999.

Rando, Therese A., PhD. "Anticipatory Grief: The Term is a Misnomer but the Phenomenon Exists," *Journal of Palliative Care*, May 1988, pp. 70-73.

Rando, Therese A., PhD. *Grief, Dying, and Death: Clinical Interventions for Caregivers.* Champaign, IL: Research Press Company, pp. 18-19, 36-39, 60, 93-104, 208-210.

Rando, Therese A., PhD. *Loss & Anticipatory Grief.* New York: Lexington Books, MacMillan, Inc., 1986, pp. 18-25, 63-79, 104.

Roberts, Cokie and Roberts, Steven V. "Puppy Love: the Final Days of a Bedraggled and Beloved Old Basset Hound," *USA Weekend*, April 9-11, 1999, p. 25.

Rollin, Betty. "Quiet Triumphs" television program, June 14, 1999.

Rosen, Elliott. *Families Facing Death.* Lexington, MA: D. C. Heath and Company, 1990, pp. 94-98.

Showalter, Sherry, MSW. "Walking with Grief: The Trail of Tears in a World of AIDS," *The American Journal of Hospice & Palliative Care*, March/April 1997, pp. 68-74.

Stolle, Matthew. "Giving Hope to Others," *Post-Bulletin*, June 4, 2001, p. 1A.

Tatelbaum, Judy. *The Courage to Grieve: Creative Living, Recovery & Growth Through Grief.* New York: Harper & Row, 1980, pp. 9-10, 15, 29-31, 50.

Turkoski, Beatrice, RN, PHD and Lance, Brenda, RN, MSN. "The Use of Guided Imagery with Anticipatory Grief," *Home Healthcare Nurse*, volume 14, number 11, 1996, pp. 878-888.

University of Minnesota Extension Service, "Who Gets Grandma's Yellow Pie Plate?" brochure, December 1999.

Veniga, Robert, MD. *A Gift of Hope: How We Survive Our Tragedies.* Boston: Little, Brown and Company, 1985, pp. 26, 108-109, 215, 232.

Ventura, Michael. "The Clinical Lessons of 9/11," *Psychotherapy Network*, September/October 2002, pp. 50-52, 70.

Volkan, Vamik D., MD and Zintl, Elizabeth. *Life After Loss: The Lessons of Grief.* New York: Charles Scribner's Sons, 1993, pp. 53, 100.

Walker, Rebecca J., PhD et al. "Anticipatory Grief and AIDS: Strategies for Intervening with Caregivers," *Health and Social Work*, February 1996, pp. 49-57.

Wall, Steve and Arden, Harvey. *Wisdomkeepers: Meetings with Native American Spiritual Elders.* Hillsboro, OR: Beyond Words Publishing, Inc., 1990, p.19.

Walsh, Froma and McGoldrick, Monica, Editors. *Living Beyond Loss: Death in the Family.* New York: W. W. Norton & Company, pp. 9, 144-162.

Weiss, John. "Care for Life: Hospice Brings Comfort, Security to Dying," *Post-Bulletin*, January 27, 2001, pp. 4B-5B.

Weiss, John. "Hospice: A Return to Old Ways," *Post-Bulletin*, January 27, 2001, p. 1B.

Welch, Deborah, RN, MSN. "Anticipatory Grief Reactions in Family Members of Adult Patients," *Issues in Mental Health Nursing*, volume 4, 1982, pp. 149-158.

Westberg, Granger E. *Good Grief.* Philadelphia: Fortress Press, 1971, p. 9.

Wolfeldt, Alan D., PhD. "A Nation Mourns: Understanding Personal Symptoms of Trauma," www.centerforloss.com/centerpiece4.html.

Yoll, James W., SRN, ONC. "The Bridge Beyond: Strengthening Nursing Practice in Attitudes Toward Death, Dying, the Terminally Ill, and Helping Spouses of Critically Ill Patients," *Intensive Care Nursing,* June 1989, pp. 88-94.

ABOUT THE AUTHORS

HARRIET HODGSON

Harriet Hodgson has been a nonfiction writer for 26 years. She graduated with honors from Wheelock College, earning a BS in Early Childhood Education, and has an MA in Art Education from the University of

Minnesota. After teaching for a dozen years she changed careers and turned to writing.

Hodgson is the author of 24 books for parents and children. Her recent work focuses on health and she is a member of the Association of Health Care Journalists. Hodgson has appeared on more than 135 radio talk shows, including CBS, and many television networks, including CNN. She is cited in the library reference, *Something About the Author*, and *Who's Who in American Women*.

The mother of two grown daughters and grandmother of twins, Hodgson lives in Rochester, MN with her husband, John. To learn more about her work go to www.harriethodgson.com.

LOIS KRAHN

Dr. Lois Krahn has been a psychiatrist and sleep medicine specialist since completing her postgraduate training in 1994. She has an AB Cum Laude from Bryn Mawr College in Bryn Mawr, PA and an MD from the Mayo Clinic College of Medicine in Rochester, MN.

HARRIET HODGSON, BS, MA & LOIS KRAHN, MD

A well-rounded physician, Dr. Krahn has an active Mayo Clinic practice in psychiatry and sleep medicine. She chairs the Department of Psychiatry at Mayo Clinic in Scottsdale, Arizona, where she teaches medical students, allied health staff and residents, and continuing education courses for physicians. She has written 42 scholarly articles on psychiatric and sleep topics. In 2001 Mayo Clinic named her an Associate Professor of Psychiatry.

Dr. Krahn is married to a physician who is employed at Mayo Clinic. Their family consists of two young children and a Golden Retriever.

Index

activities, 6
adaptational tasks, 57-58
age factor, 55-56
anger, 91-92
cathexis, 149
changes
   appearance, 39-40
   behavior, 85-86
   health, 87-88
   life-altering, 44-45
   place, 35-36
   position, 38-39
children's grief, 13-14, 22, 27
chronic grief, 113-114
communicating
   with children, 27-28
   with family, 75
   with siblings, 105-106
community services, 146
complexity of early grief, 9-10
conspiracy of silence, 133-134
coping
   approach, 124-125
   with change, 48-49
   with suspense and fear, 28-29,
counseling, 46, 130-132
crisis, 25-26
crying, 123-124
death
   appropriate, 147-148

child's, 56
  parent's, 55-56
  sibling's, 56-57
  view of, 147, 150
decathexis
  definition, 117
  early, 117-118
  systemic, 118-119
delayed grief, 77-78
denial, 90-91
depression
  early signs, 98-99
  in parents of HIV/AIDS patients, 111
  symptoms, 99-100
detachment, 88-89
details, missing, 95-96
dividing the goods, 107-109
early grief symptoms, 69-70
emotions
  conflicting, 62
  emotional limbo, 7
  emotional pain, 114-115
  hiding, 92-93
  rehearsing, 141-143
  releasing, 74
empathy, 145-146
endpoint of early grief, 11-12
experience
  too little, 60
  too much, 61-62
family
  culture/customs, 64

   history, 144
   loyalty/closeness, 143
   relationships, 106-107
   resentment, 79
   roles, 58-59
   system, 37-38, 74-75
   workshops, 46
fear
   of going crazy, 93
   of terrorism, 23-24
finances, 74, 115-116
flat affect, 86
focuses of early grief, 4-5
goals, new, 134-135
good from grief, making, 152-153
grief triggers, 63
grieving styles
   activist, 79-80
   "crazyperson," 79
   hero, 78
   martyr, 79
   personal, 80
   super-responsible, 79
guided imagery, 131-132
guilt
   personal, 5, 6, 56, 132
   intervention, 62
healing path, 154-155
health, personal, 39-40, 87-88
health professionals' early grief, 47-48
HIV/AIDS, 110-113
hope, 3, 10-11, 31, 154

hospice, 15, 41, 46, 80, 91, 95, 114
information, finding, 91
isolation/aloneness, 80
journal writing, 126-128
joy, 23
laughter, 132-133
legal protection, 109-110
life on hold, 93-95
listening to the sick and dying, 129-130
living-dying interval, 72-74
loss, 61-62, 112-113
measuring early grief
   loss history graph, 61-62
   "The 10-Mile Mourning Bridge," 41-42
moment, living the, 149-151
needs
   identifying, 128-129
   ignoring, 96-97
overriding emotions, 92
panic, 88
personality
   strengths, 55
   types, 53-55
pet(s), 40
post-death grief, 151-152
preparation work, 135-136
priorities, 148-149
reality
   accepting, 45-46
   loss of, 97-98
recurring early grief, 75-55
relationship

with family, 106-107
  with partner, 77, 107
  with ill person, 56-57
religious/spiritual beliefs, 65, 137-138
reorganization, 144-145
responses
  to early grief, 85
  extreme, 100-101
Resurrection-of-the-Dead Syndrome, 116-117
routine, 125-126
safe retreats, 86
self-grief, 43, 116, 143
September 11th, 21-22
shock, 12, 159
sibling rivalry, 105-106
social contacts, 86-87
stages of early grief, 70-72
stigma of disease, 110-112
sublimation, 95
suspense and fear, 8-9, 28-29
support, 14-15, 72
surrogate grievors, 47-48
terrorism
  burden of, 25-26
  confronting, 24-25
  coping with, 28-29
  early grief of, 21, 70
  plan, 30-31
  scope of, 26-27
  talking with children about, 27-28
time
  adjustment time, 30

    factor, 7-8
    gift and enemy, 90
    making the most of, 8
    shifts, 22-24
trauma, 21
uncompleted loss, 5
uniqueness of early grief, 12
vulnerability, 42-43